mini house style

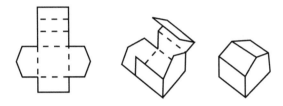

mini house style

ricorico

HARPER
DESIGN

An Imprint of HarperCollinsPublishers

STAFF

Advisor: Rikuo Nishimori

Material research: NAA (Soichiro Ando, Rie Asano, Tetsuhito Takata), Alma Reyes-Umemoto

English translation and copyediting: Keiko Kitamura, Alma Reyes-Umemoto

Art direction and layout: Eiko Nishida/cooltiger

Chief editor and producer: Rico Komanoya

First published in 2004 by:
Harper Design International, an imprint of HarperCollins Publishers
10 East 53rd Street
New York, NY 10022

Distributed throughout the world by:
HarperCollins International
10 East 53rd Street
New York, NY 10022
Tel.: (212) 207-7000
Fax: (212) 207-7654
www.harpercollins.com

HarperCollins books may be purchased for educational, business, or sales promotional
use. For information, please write: Special Markets Department, HarperCollins Publishers Inc.,
10 East 53rd Street, New York, NY 10022

Library of Congress Cataloging-in-Publication Data

Komanoya, Rico.
    Mini house style / by Rico Komanoya.
    p. cm.
    Includes index.
    ISBN 0-06-058907-8 (hardcover)
    1. Small houses.   I. Title.
NA7533.K66 2004
728'.37--dc22

2004014893

DL: B-26752-04

Printed by: Anman Gràfiques del Vallès, Sabadell, Spain

First Printing, 2004

MINI HOUSE STYLE: CONTENTS

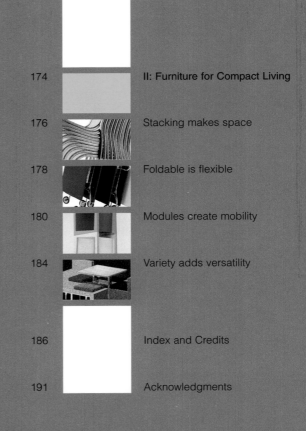

INTRODUCTION

The Birth of the Mini House Style

by Rikuo Nishimori, NAA

There is no doubt that the decreased number of family members per house unit and the increased need for housing for individuals rather than entire families are the major causes of the current mini house boom. Added to that is the fact that urban lifestyles have been changing over the last few decades. Because of the homogenization of information and rapid economic change, the construction of the city as a physical space is no longer able to keep up with these changes. Domestic architecture, therefore, is the unit most able to respond quickly to change and may be the building type most suitable to cope with these phenomena.

Moreover, small houses arouse much attention and are in demand not only in cramped cities such as Tokyo and London, but also in the more spacious cities of North America and Northern Europe. This phenomenon shows that the trend has been caused by the residents' needs as well as their external circumstances. In other words, the value of the house as a symbol of the family is obsolete. The architectural borderline between housing and other building styles has now become less clear-cut, with houses combining business functions and requirements for comfortable life in a small space. Similarly, the social nature of housing as a property has been reduced while the individual characteristics have increased. In these circumstances, young architects who create continuously innovative housing styles assume vital roles in mini house architecture.

In the 20th century, when architecture adopted the important strategy called Modernism, architects created nonmonumental buildings one after another. These were rather large-scale public buildings and city planning projects. However, mini houses gradually attracted public attention (e.g., Le Corbusier's "Mother's House" and Jean Prouvé's "l'École de Nancy"). Various backgrounds also influenced the construction of mini house projects, such as the revamping of traditional vernacular huts and townhouses and the rise of industrial and prefabricated units. At the same time, in the current of Modernism, which embodies design concepts in their purest form, mini houses are no longer the peripheral subjects of discussion; instead, they have become the core. This can be illustrated through the representative works of world-famous Japanese architects Tadao Ando and Toyo Ito, who have been recognized as innovators of small-scale houses. This style, which is an integral work of architecture, is the most appropriate building form to express the specific and essential concept of space.

In order to understand the essential qualities of most mini houses introduced in this book, we also have to learn about their concepts. For instance, a small, isolated hut in an open field and a constricted mini house in a narrow tract each have distinct backgrounds. Architectural design is based on consistent needs, the history of the site, and the site's environmental context. Therefore, each building is unique and tells us about the present nature of the society and the city in which we live. It may also give us clues to our future. The realistic or "structuralistic" architectural style is pragmatized through the need for minimization, which never applies to large, expensive mansions or expanded country houses. We can see, therefore, the unique relationship between the house and its owner through the space from which the arbitrary marks are eliminated.

We enjoy building houses for individuals in a new society that is free from obsolete language, such as "mass-market" and "nation states." Mini houses, which are no longer social properties, are always within close reach, meaning that this housing style has become increasingly popular. We can see the edge of this trend in the mini house projects presented in this book. They do not signify prototypes of Modernism, but rather respond to the various needs of urban people. The "9tubo-house/Sumire Aoi House" project, designed to fit into current lifestyles, adopted exactly the skeleton of Makoto Masuzawa's "Small Scale House," which was built 50 years ago. It is an ample demonstration of how simple and versatile this architectural form is. This kind of experiment could be an important catalyst to bridge the diminishing gap between the industrial or commercial house and the architect's own desire. It suggests the birth of a new style that will eventually lead to the creation of a new function for architects.

"Small-scale housing forms what one could call the undergrowth of dwelling from which thoughts about the world are to germinate. One of the most important tasks for these pioneer species of architecture is to create possibilities for a balanced and interactive relationship between man and nature. It requires discarding anthropocentric thinking and understanding the inherent value of nature itself. It also means renewing the concept of time in architecture. The mini house style is typically characterized by a holistic approach and an inbuilt ephemerality. This offers a good basis both to renew architecture towards more sustainable solutions as well as to conceive a home or a housing area as an ever-changing built landscape. If small-scale projects help us to understand buildings as momentary, they also make it possible to manifest an attitude about life spans that link both the building methods and the ways of living. At the same time, the adaptability and possibility to complement a home so that it more easily corresponds with the changing situation and the individual needs of the resident may become a natural part of building houses."

— *Markku Hedman*, Architects M.H. Coop

We have gathered a number of mini house projects from all over the world that represent how architects are rising to the challenge and using previously unimaginable design methods to satisfy the needs of compact living. Both existing and prototypical projects are accompanied by the architects' own professional views and opinions about the essence and relevance of living in the mini house style.

ALL ABOUT MINI HOUSES

Casa Bola can be called a Spherical Housing System. The sphere, a potent symbol, is the volume with the least surface area and thus demands the less building material. When compared to a cube of the same volume, the sphere requires 19 percent less external surface material, resulting in a ratio of almost six spheres to five cubes. In order to be industrialized, transported, and plugged in, the modular house should be lightweight, and the sphere, like a bubble, is the lightest shape. A freestanding house is surely more expensive than a conventional one, but if price were the only issue, freestanding houses would not exist. In today's crowded city environment, however, the freestanding house provides designers with a more humane, less invasive, and altogether priceless solution to urbanisitic design.

Casa Bola

Year: Redecorated, repainted 2004 · Location: São Paulo, Brazil · Floor Area: 1,076 square feet · Architect: Eduardo Longo/Eduardo Longo Arquitetura · Photographers: Fausto Ivan, Ana Carvalho

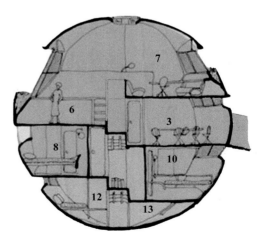

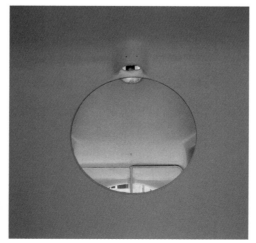

Can you describe briefly the design concept behind the project and the reason for its compactness?

This "ball house" is a mockup, a big scale model of a "plug-in" residence. Its diameter is 26.24 feet smaller than the ideal 32.81 feet for a full-scale prototype, which is the width of the house on top of which it stands. That is the reason why it is so compact. The main purpose of this project is to create a new kind of elongated, high-rise building, formed by several spherical units, plugged in to a megastructure containing the vertical and horizontal accesses (elevators, ramps, stairs, and skywalks).

The innovative concept in this project is its empty spaces between the spheres, which create "free-standing" residential units, allowing, from the individual point of view, independence and privacy. From the collective point of view, these empty spaces allow the flow of air, light, and vision, resulting in a new typology of large architectonical structures that offer a more transparent, humane, and less invasive solution to urbanistic design.

What is the most striking feature/element of this project that you believe makes it unique from other small-scale houses?

It is sufficiently unique due to its spherical shape, but what is striking or even surprising for visitors is how "spacious" it is inside, compared to what is expected when observed from the outside. That is probably because a sphere has no sharp, defining edges. Also, when judging the size of a regular house, one usually looks at how wide it is. A sphere is equally wide, high, and deep, thus not registering its actual volume in the eye of the observer.

If you were to lay down Five Commandments for effective compact architectural design, what would these be? Relate also how each commandment is fulfilled in the project.

1) Use rounded corners and edges to disguise spatial limits, granting the sensation of continuity.
2) Use light colors to enlarge rooms.
3) Remember that small-proportioned windows create claustrophobic rooms; large ones make rooms small—the ball house migrated from tiny to large openings until a proper size was achieved.
4) Apply smoothly finished surfaces to avoid the sensation of discomfort.
5) Do not collect unnecessary objects.

The sphere is the volume with the least surface area.

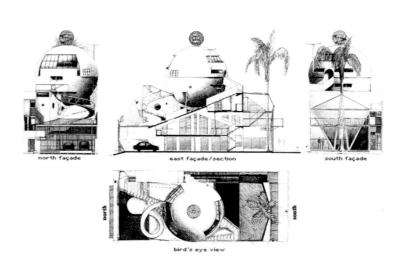

north façade   east façade/section   south façade

bird's eye view

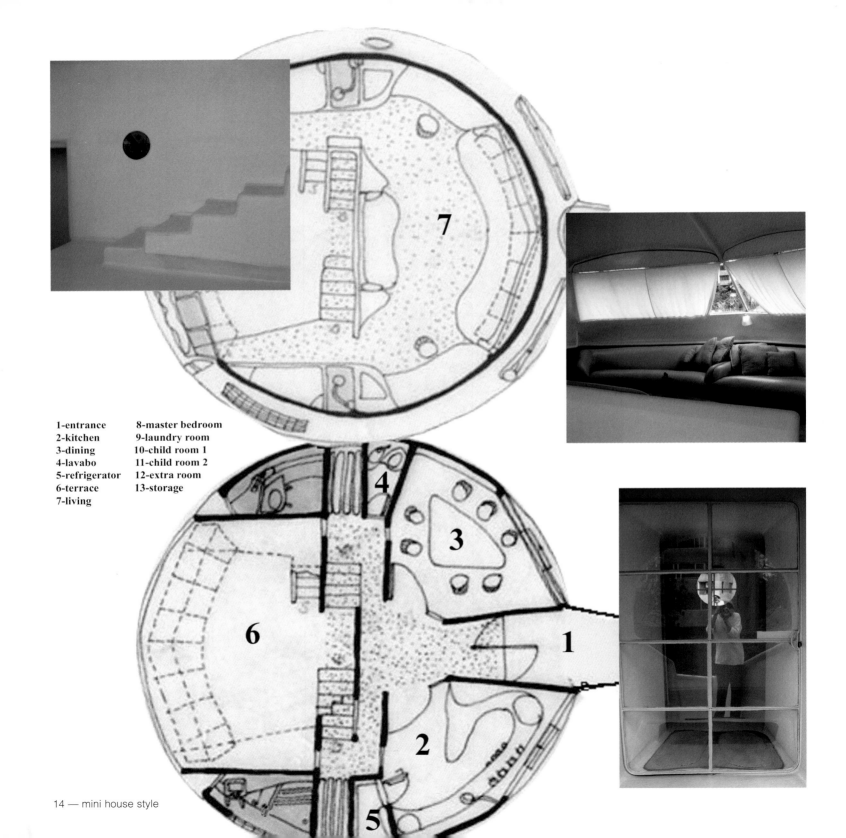

1-entrance
2-kitchen
3-dining
4-lavabo
5-refrigerator
6-terrace
7-living

8-master bedroom
9-laundry room
10-child room 1
11-child room 2
12-extra room
13-storage

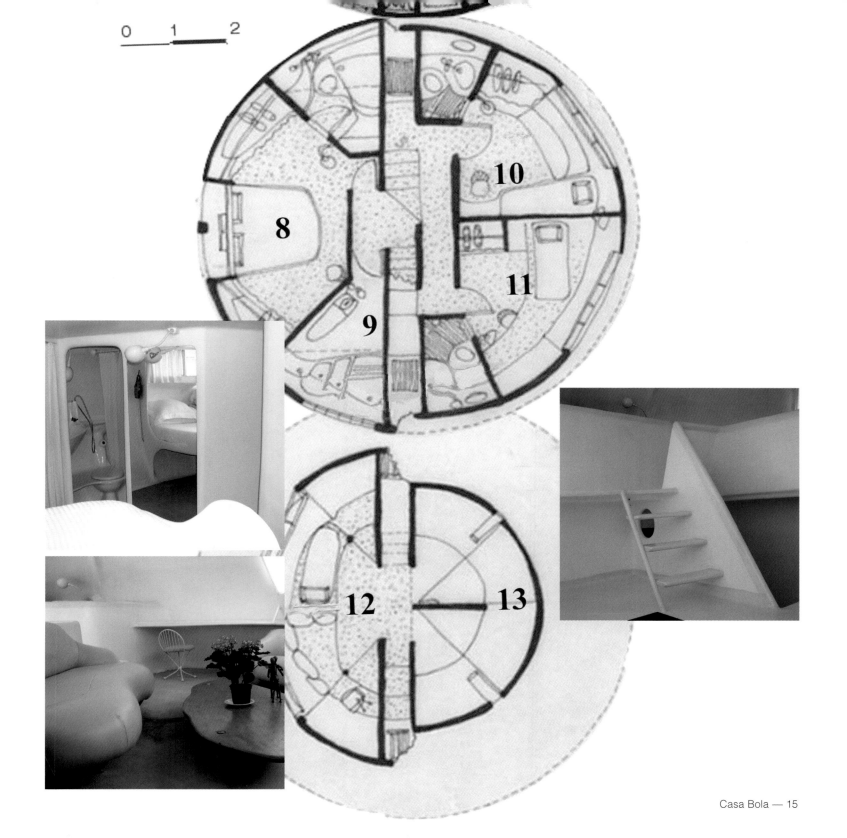

The holiday cottage sits on a plot area of 6,778.80 square feet in Flumserberg, Switzerland. Most holiday resorts look the same, like housing estates everywhere. The homeowners live on their own piece of land, in a house surrounded by a flat garden. The topography of the site and the qualities of the place are rarely acknowledged. The houses look like they came straight from the catalog of a prefabricated home. What is the difference between everyday living and temporary holiday living? Even when building a vacation home, most people still stay on safe ground. The vacation home is all too often just a trimmed-down version of the prototypical one-family home. The chance to break away from everyday routine, to really live differently in the holidays, is frequently missed. This holiday cottage seizes the opportunity for innovation with its vertical and horizontal zones, creating a living space where every zone serves multiple purposes.

Vacation Cottage

Year: 2003 • Location: Flumserberg, Switzerland • Floor Area: 1,119.04 square feet • Architects: Mathias Müller, Daniel Niggli, Christoph Rothenhoefer/EM2N Architekten ETH/SIA • Photographer: Hannes Henz

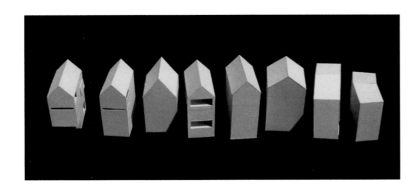

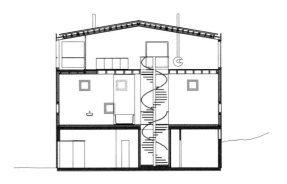

Can you describe briefly the design concept behind the project and the reason for its compactness?

Chalet and Tower

Our design refuses to accept the leveling colonization of the territory. It assumes a position: sited next to an alpine pasture, which in winter serves as a ski slope, the house rises up high to catch the sun and the spectacular views on all sides. At the same time, it establishes a dialogue with the place: around the house, the alpine pasture remains intact. In winter, the neighbors can ski across the lot towards the ski slope. The border of the lot isn't marked, and the volume of the house bends in order to welcome the swing of the hillside. The exterior develops the omnipresent theme of the low, wide chalet house with dark wooden cladding and small windows into the image of a dark wooden tower with great openings.

What is the most striking feature/element of this project that you believe makes it unique from other small-scale houses?

Vacation living

We based our design on the thesis of the one-room house as an antithesis to everyday living in closed-off rooms. There are no rooms, just vertical and horizontal zones; every zone serves multiple purposes. The garage was developed to be an outdoor-indoor playroom in summer; the sleeping floor accommodates up to eight people in one large, double-height open space—it also serves as a bathroom; the bathtub and the spiral stairs divide this space into two zones. On the living floor, which reads like a miniature house with its pitched roof, the kitchen and fireplace divide the space. There is a spatial progression from the dark, artificially lit garage, to the sleeping floor with its small window proportions, to the light-flooded living floor with views into the surrounding landscape.

Economic building

The luxury of this house lies in its site and spaces, not in expensive details and materials. In order to meet the budget, we had to focus on certain concerns: we kept the windows on the sleeping floor as small as possible (minimal window surface was required by the zoning laws) in order to be able to pay for the extra-large windows on the living floor; in close cooperation with the wood-building engineer, we looked for the cheapest construction for floors, outer walls, and roof; the laws required us to build a garage. We treated the surface of the concrete walls with a special surface obtained by nailing a drain mat commonly used on the outside of basements into the concrete formwork—this surface turns a concrete box into a poetic, cave-like indoor-outdoor space.

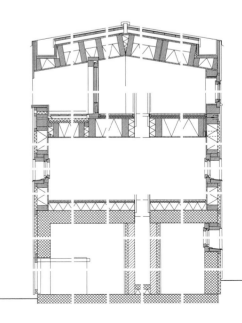

If you were to lay down Five Commandments for effective compact architectural design, what would these be? Relate also how each commandment is fulfilled in the project.

1) Compensate for lack of size; create maximum spatial richness and diversity.
2) Give the small volume strength; create a strong shape that makes for identity.
3) Avoid cartoonlike oversimplification; create ambiguous shapes with multiple possible readings; to optimize the usability of the small house, create rooms that allow for many different modes of use and are open to interpretation.
4) A small house cannot fulfill all the wishes of the client and the architect, so you have to make some tough choices and prioritize decisions. Minimize certain elements in order to maximize others.
5) Compact houses lend themselves to experimentation with the brief, the spaces, the materials—seize the opportunities of smallness and have fun.

Create ambiguous shapes with multiple possible readings.

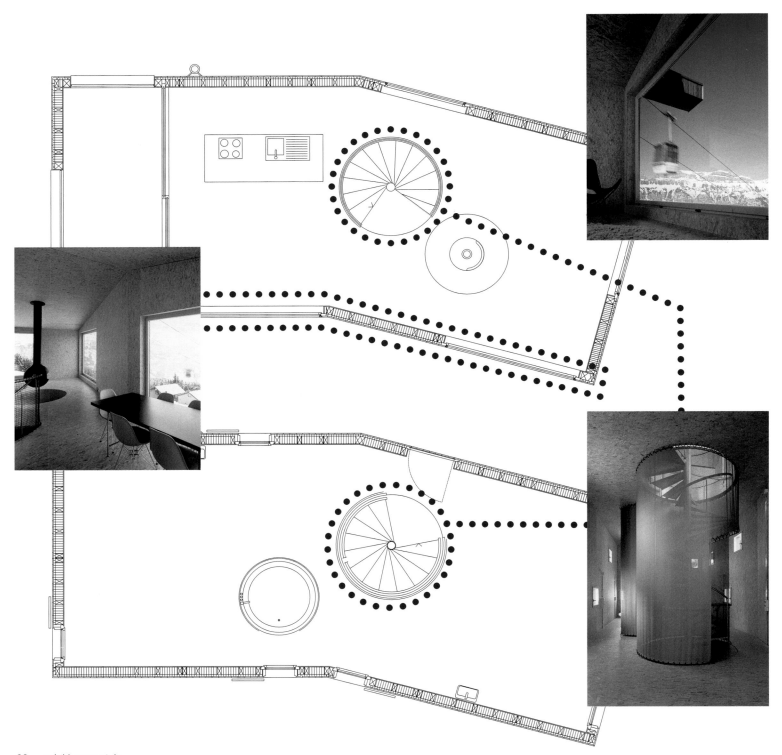

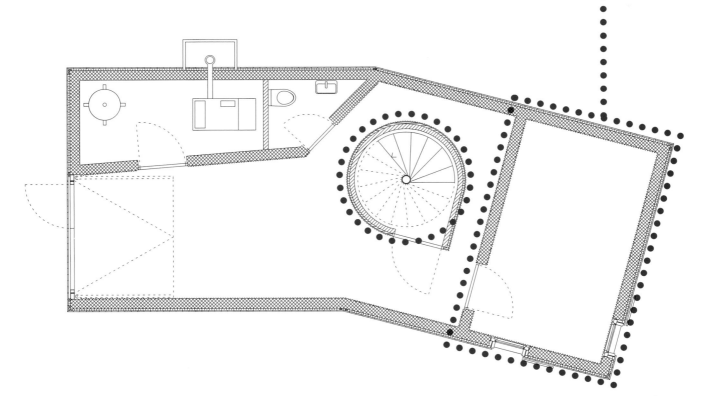

This small weekend house contains an entry, a living/dining room, a kitchen on the first floor, as well as two rooms and a shower on the upper level. With the exception of the concrete posts, the entire house is made of wood: the load-bearing structure is pine, the inner walls and floors are triple-ply boards, and the façade is made of larch cladding. With its respect for the site and its adherence to natural construction materials, the house provides its inhabitants with a harmonious weekend getaway.

House Campo Vallemaggia

Year: 1998 • Location: Campo Vallemaggia, Switzerland • Floor Area: 408.88 square feet • Architect: Roberto Briccola

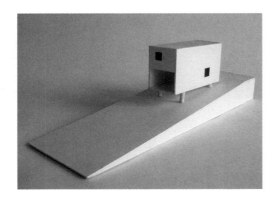

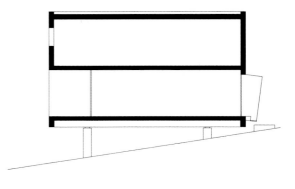

Can you describe briefly the design concept behind the project and the reason for its compactness?

This small house was intentionally designed to respect the site and its characteristics. The cube raised on posts is a modern way of playing with a traditional Walser granary (the Walser was a group of German-speaking Swiss who migrated into what is now Italian-speaking Switzerland in the 13th century). In this way, the terrain beneath the house remains untouched. The site of the house made it possible to build additional buildings in the future. The view from the window reveals the neighboring village and the silhouette of the mountains.

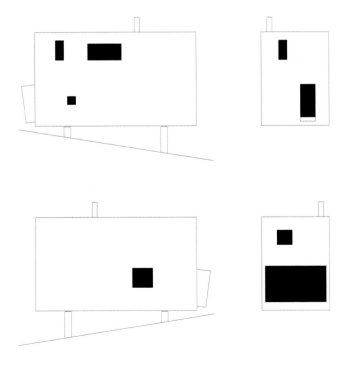

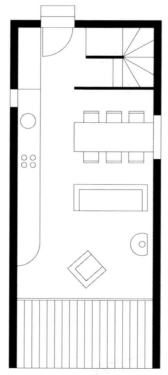

Under the house the flowers grow!

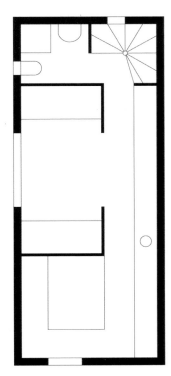

What is the most striking feature/element of this project that you believe makes it unique from other small-scale houses?

The absolute respect to the site is the most striking feature. Under the house the flowers grow!

If you were to lay down Five Commandments for effective compact architectural design, what would these be? Relate also how each commandment is fulfilled in the project.

1) The area should be small.
2) The cost should be cheap and the structure easy to build.
3) There should be minimum occupation of the lot.
4) The design must respect the site.
5) It should be possible to repeat the same typology.

The 9tubohouse is the product of a new design housing concept initiated by architect and designer Makoto Masuzawa and based on his introduction of small-scale houses. Other architects and designers were attracted to this concept of "remaking" (remodeling) design by adhering to design principles rather than demands of commercial housing. The 9tubohouse is not based on traditional housing. Instead, the architect, Makoto Koizumi, focuses on strict design considerations that allow the users to respond to better lifestyles and space concepts.

9tubohouse/Sumire Aoi House

Year: 2002 • Location: Tokyo, Japan • Floor Area: 533.37 square feet • Architect: Makoto Koizumi • Photographers: Yuri Hagiwara, Soichi Murazumi, Nacása & Partners Inc.

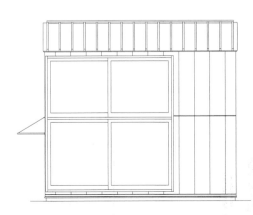

32 — mini house style

Can you describe briefly the design concept behind the project and the reason for its compactness?

The original prototype for this project stemmed from Makoto Masuzawa's design of his own house 50 years ago: a small-scale residence built for a family of four. The name, "tubo," is derived from the Japanese unit of building measurement, "tsubo," which is equivalent to 35.50 square feet. Five design rules were applied to the design of this project:

1) use of a 3 "tsubo" x 3 "tsubo" (3 x 35.50 square feet) space planning concept.
2) vertical volume of 3 "tsubo" (3 x 35.50 square feet).
3) use of traditional Japanese roofing.
4) use of round pillars.
5) use of open main façade.

What is the most striking feature/element of this project that you believe makes it unique from other small-scale houses?

The plan is based on strict design principles rather than commercial demand. It follows the philosophy of "remaking" design in order to generate creativity.

If you were to lay down Five Commandments for effective compact architectural design, what would these be? Relate also how each commandment is fulfilled in the project.

1) New movements in the design industry lead to new architectural creation: treat housing as a product design.
2) "Remake" (remodel) design to generate creativity.
3) Instill originality while shrinking the dimensions to bring about a new design.
4) Offer simple purchase power to users.
5) Focus on design rather than commercial demand.

The plan follows the philosophy of "remaking" design.

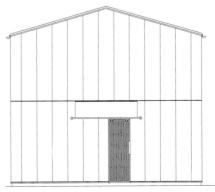

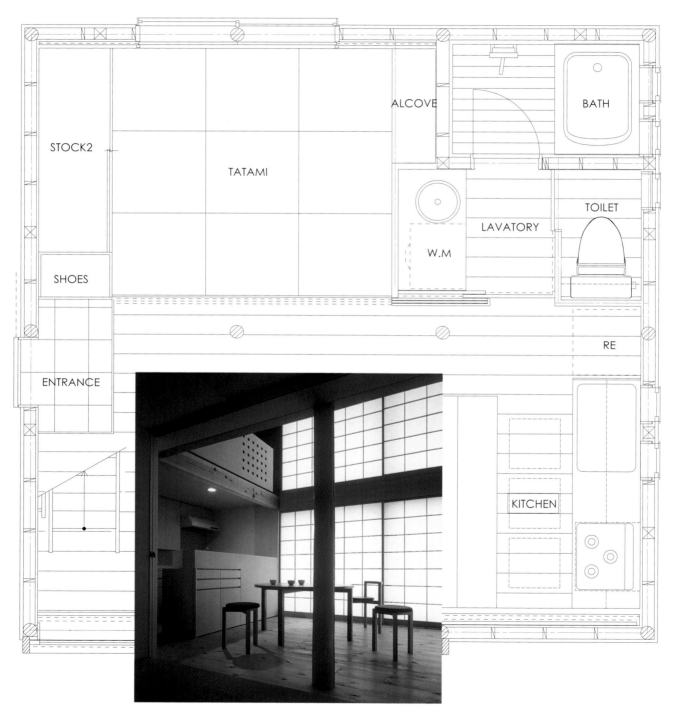

STOCK2

TATAMI

ALCOVE

BATH

SHOES

W.M

LAVATORY

TOILET

ENTRANCE

RE

KITCHEN

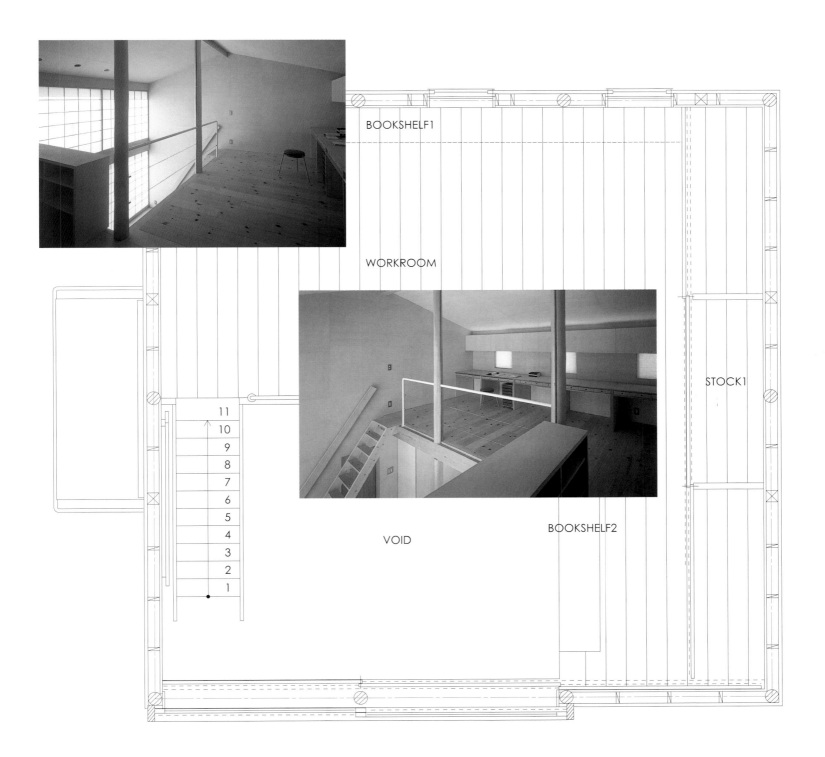

BOOKSHELF1

WORKROOM

STOCK1

11
10
9
8
7
6
5
4
3
2
1

VOID

BOOKSHELF2

This project converted a simple, isolated farm-house into a holiday home. Because the quarry stone house was in a ruinous state, without sanitary facilities, the primary objectives of the design were the reconstruction of the structure and the installation of a kitchen and a bathroom. The concept behind the new part of the building was to create authentic architectures that would permit clear associations and images and satisfy the expectations of holiday atmospheres.

Obviously, a purely functional conversion would not be satisfactory, so the resulting task was to create a combination of extreme atmospheres, a transition between the old building and the new that would appear nostalgic while meeting the owner's demands for originality. The result is a holiday home that meets the needs of any occasion.

À Nous de Choisir

Year: 1995 • Location: Normandy, France • Floor Area: 2,033.64 square feet •
Architects: Gerhard Kalhöfer, Christele Jany/Kalhöfer-Korschildgen Architekten • Photographers: Rolf Brunsendorf, Stefan Thurman

Can you describe briefly the design concept behind the project and the reason for its compactness?

The concept proposes the creation of two independent tracts of different characters. Space, light, materials, and coloration were to provide the occupants with fundamentally different feelings and choices.

After surveying the remaining structure and removing the damage to the roof and ceiling, the old building was reconstructed, reusing much of the existing fabric. The result was supposed to meet the owner's nostalgic demands and appear original, rather than resemble a museum.

The closed, historical building was extended with a separate modern part. The extension houses all necessary modern comforts in compact form, compressing the service facilities into just a few elements. The design creates flowing transitions between the inside and the outside within a holiday home that can be used in different ways, depending on the season.

What is the most striking feature/element of this project that you believe makes it unique from other small-scale houses?

During the summer, life can expand into the landscape (meadow and pond), since the steel framework contains also an outdoor shower and a toilet. The boundaries between inside and outside are dissolved as a result of large areas of glazing. An optional screen was applied instead of a fixed spatial separation of the kitchen and bathroom. At night, the flow of the steel structure is revealed by the use of ship's lamps, which highlight the individual functional cells. In contrast to the old part of the building, the materials used in the extension are almost exclusively industrially manufactured articles, such as coarse chipboard, plywood, industrial tarpaulin, and perforated sheet metal. The colors symbolize the various functions: kitchen, bathroom, etc. All technical services (water and gas) are installed independently. Two spaces, two alternatives—we have the choice to rest or to take another step ahead: à nous de choisir.

If you were to lay down Five Commandments for effective compact architectural design, what would these be? Relate also how each commandment is fulfilled in the project.

1) Use logical zoning and a reflected relationship among spaces—this house has two clear zones with inside-outside relationships.
2) Have multi-interpretative spaces and objects.
3) Use multifunctional spaces and objects—the living space is open and functional.
4) Allow spaces to have optional uses.
5) Make use of spaces in between rooms—the spaces in the houses are organized.

Life can expand into the landscape.

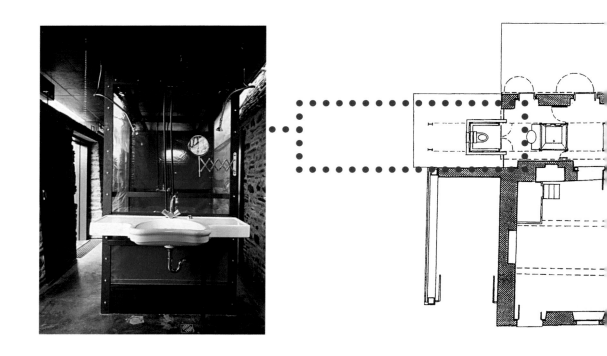

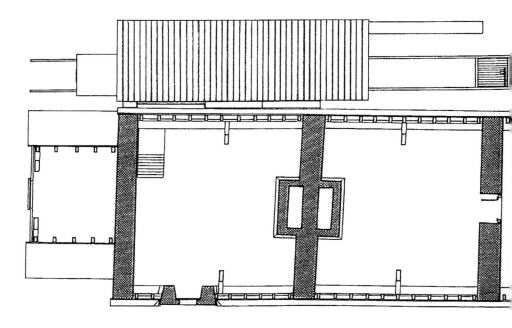

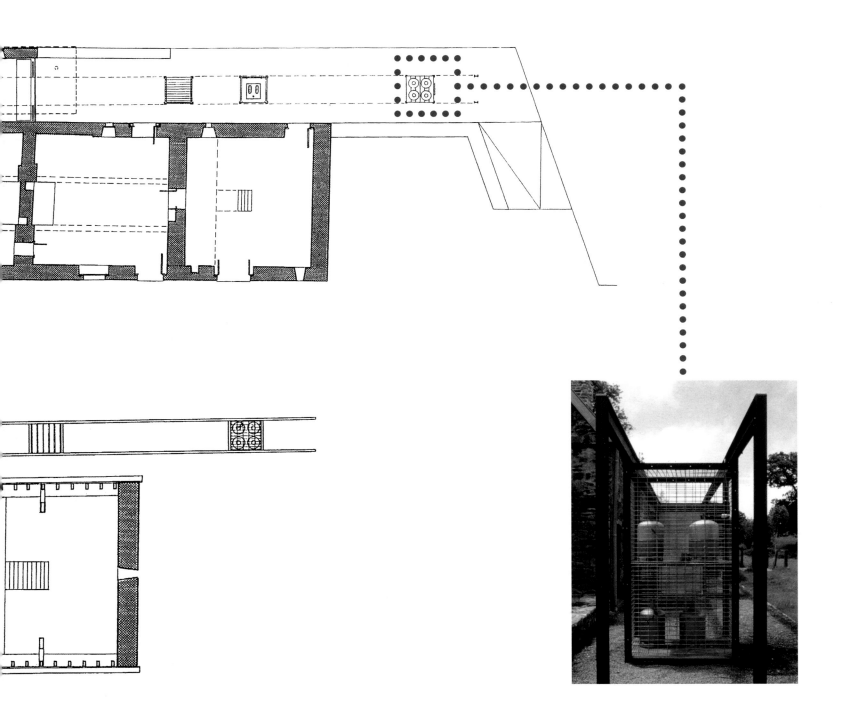

The project name, Gucklhupf, originates from the name of a hill near the site, Guglhupf, which in turn refers to a typical Austrian cake, served on Sundays and called "Gucklhupf." Both terms derive from the verbs *gucken* and *hüpfen*, which indicate the actions of watching and hopping up and down in an attempt to find a better vantage point.

The Gucklhupf was designed for the 1993 Festival of the Regions in northern Austria as a cultural, artistic, and architectural manifestation meant to evoke a "strange" appeal. Built by Wörndl himself, along with two collaborators, it is a metaphorical object positioned on a plot of land beside the Mondsee Lake. The design caused much controversy among local authorities and inhabitants because of the inherent tension between the strange and the familiar. It nevertheless attained its purpose of not achieving a final state, but instead exists as a live object that remains in a state of permanent transformation, even after its supposed completion.

Gucklhupf

Year: 1993 · Location: Loibichl, Innerschwand, Mondsee, Austria · Floor Area: 516.48 square feet · Architect: Hans Peter Wörndl/Architekurbüro Hans Peter Wörndl · Photographer: Paul Ott

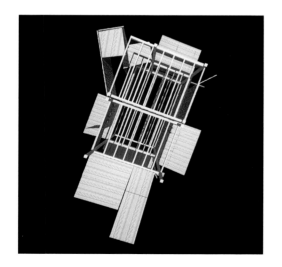

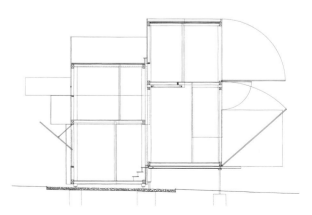

44 — mini house style

Can you describe briefly the design concept behind the project and the reason for its compactness?

The concept is based on the compact fisherman boats on the adjacent lake, built according to prehistoric, Celtic craftsmanship from one trunk of a tree. These boats have been built the same way for the past 4,000 years and are still in use (in reference to the Einbaum boat object as a kind of genius loci). Also, from a personal experience, I had won a wonderful Joe Colombo multifunctional, plastic kitchen box furniture at a MAK Design Lottery some time earlier. I tried to translate that object into a building.

With regards to the local building code, there was no building permission available for the site for political reasons. The building code includes also some aesthetic censorship. Hence, we had to develop a strategy that allowed the client to build what he wanted. We created a sculpture for a regional art festival. The site and building were open to the public part-time. The object was meant as a critique of some terrible buildings newly built close by. These buildings did, nevertheless, receive building permission because of "public interest." The rainy climate had snowy winters so the house was mainly used as a summer house. This means that the building sits in the landscape, shut down and compact during most times of the year. But it will open onto the lake, like a flower, during the warm days.

It is a live object that remains in a state of permanent transformation.

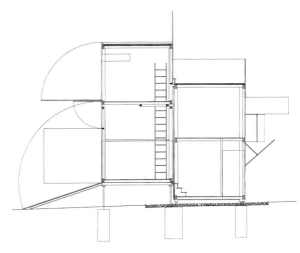

What is the most striking feature/element of this project that you believe makes it unique from other small-scale houses?

The house opens up completely towards the views, the sunlight, and the surrounding landscape. It does this through a sequence of different types of openings. In its compact state, it's a rich flower waiting to blossom.

If you were to lay down Five Commandments for effective compact architectural design, what would these be? Relate also how each commandment is fulfilled in the project.

There can be no commandments from within any architectural design concept. In my opinion, any creative work as an architect needs all freedom possibly available. Limitations are given from the specifics of a commission.

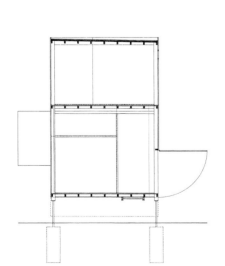
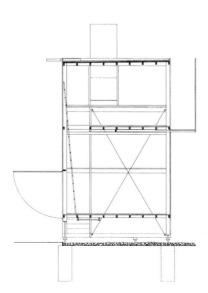
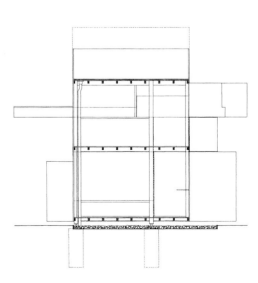

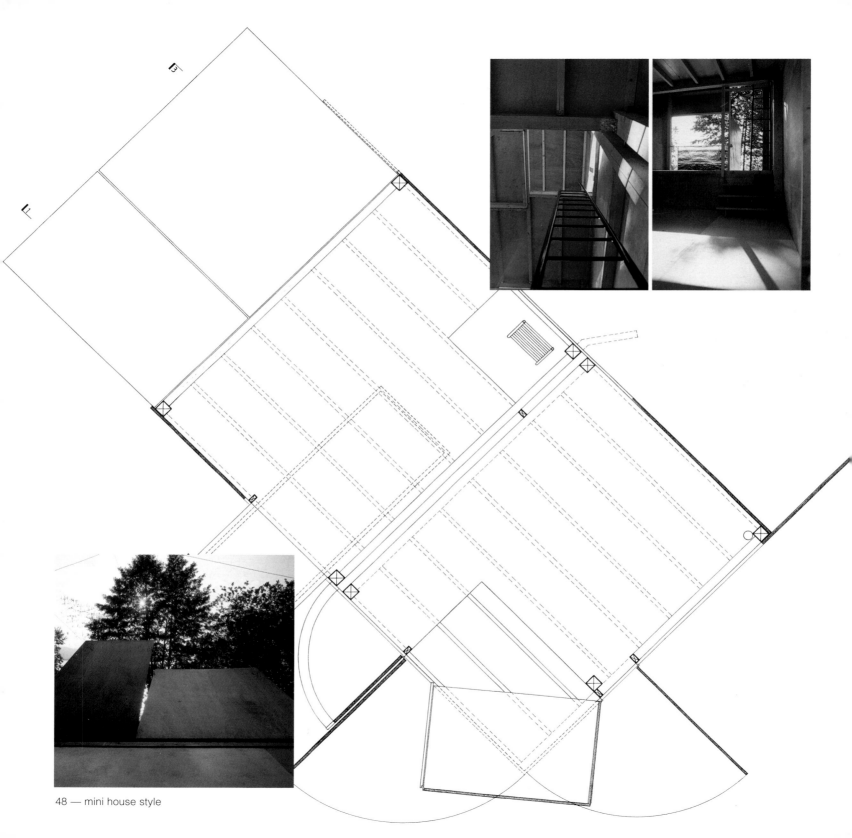

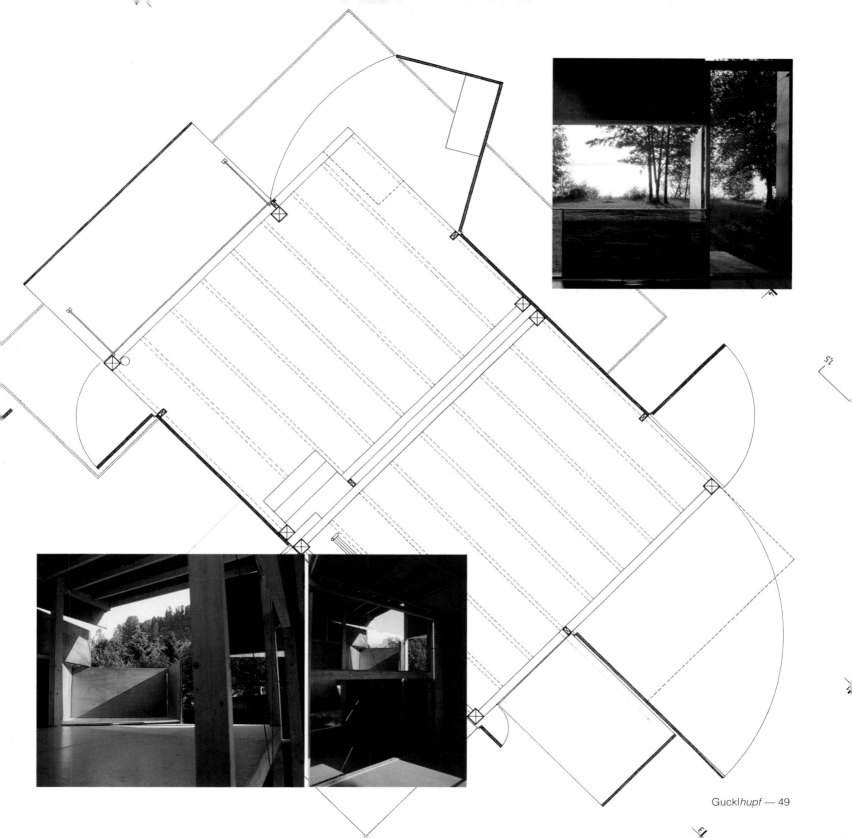

S。H。 is the product of a suburban housing style. The site, developed during the second half of the 1950s, is located in a quiet neighborhood on a hill. The clients are a married couple, both linguists from different universities. The title "S。H。" is derived from the initials of the couple's nicknames. Their shared research space, found on the ground level, was planned to occupy 30 percent of the lot—too much space for their study. Therefore, this space, which is a "dirt-floor" area called "labo" (acronym for laboratory), combined the functions of the entrance hall and the reception room. The dining room also adjoins the "labo," and the dining table doubles as a seminar table.

In the space configuration of the whole building, there are different elevations that contain two levels of five consecutively rising "skip floors." The interior looks like one huge room; it was planned this way so that the floors gradually become more private and comfortable in atmosphere as you ascend.

Consequently, there is no angle from which the whole area can be seen at the same time. The visual axis rises and falls with the iterating cycle of: "labo"↔dining room↔living room↔bedroom↔loft. The result is a unique mini house design that utilizes the most of its height and volume to create a reasonable and comfortable space.

S。H。

Year: 2003 • Location: Hyogo, Japan • Floor Area: 1,113.98 square feet • Architect: Katsuhiro Miyamoto/Katsuhiro Miyamoto & Associates • Photographer: Kei Sugino

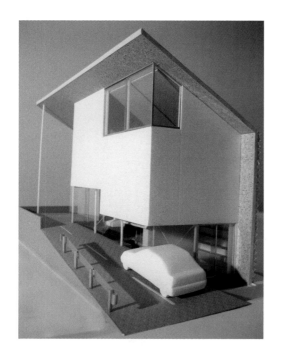

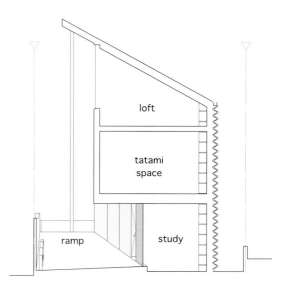

loft

tatami space

ramp

study

Can you describe briefly the design concept behind the project and the reason for its compactness?
Even though the area was very narrow, the outside space has a rich atmosphere. Moreover, it was not necessary to plan a large house for such a small family unit.

There are four stairways in this house. In response to the increasingly private atmosphere, the higher the stairway, the more gentle the angle becomes. The "white box," containing most of the private space, consists of windows that are planned in consideration of the neighboring environment and the resident's request. The "labo" nestles under the white box space, which is supported in the air by five steel columns.

There had to be plenty of storage space and shelves for the couple's everyday needs and research. The entire inside wall on the northern side functions as a versatile storage space and is an interior sequence that connects through the upper and lower floors. Its flat bars serve as bookends and partitions and also act as reinforcing elements of the architectural structure. The folded plates are placed horizontally for structural reasons on the outside of the northern wall; and to create the slit-style aperture for the light, some are replaced by FRP folded plates.

What is the most striking feature/element of this project that you believe makes it unique from other small-scale houses?
The height of the house compensates for the narrowness of the floor space. Consequently, the volume of the interior space is rather large in proportion to the floor space.

If you were to lay down Five Commandments for effective compact architectural design, what would these be? Relate also how each commandment is fulfilled in the project.
1) Understand the essential, subtle characteristics of the area.
2) Create a reasonable and comfortable space by taking full advantage of those characteristics.
3) Develop sequential spaces to reduce the narrowness by using a long flow line within a small and narrow space.
4) Pay attention to the design of the sectional plan in order to extend the height.
5) Eliminate the common and redundant elements; make the entire plan as simple as possible.

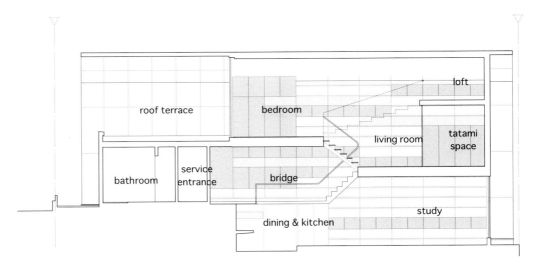

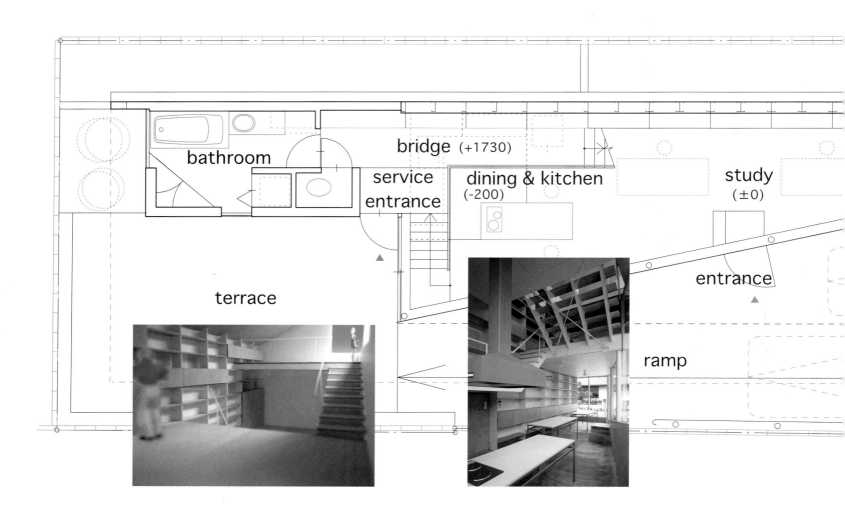

bathroom

bridge (+1730)

service
entrance

dining & kitchen
(-200)

study
(±0)

terrace

entrance

ramp

*The outside space has
a rich atmosphere.*

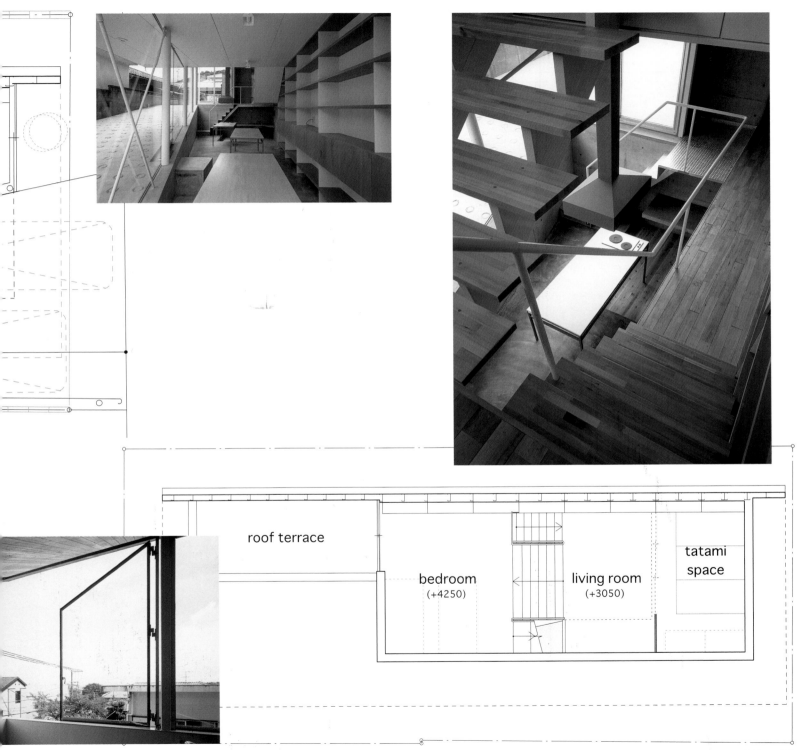

roof terrace

bedroom
(+4250)

living room
(+3050)

tatami
space

This house is located in the 19th century extension of Barcelona close to the historic center of the town, and is characterized by rectangular building blocks of one to two floors. There are houses with small patios or gardens in the interior of the block on both sides of the street. The restricted budget and the limited capacities of the available local contractors obliged the architect to stick to traditional technical and material solutions in order to avoid time and cost overrun—and also to guarantee that the house will last without great maintenance problems.

The house is closed facing the street on the north side and opens to a garden on the south side. The primary areas (living room, two bedrooms, and study) have high ceiling heights of 11.15 feet. The serving areas (kitchen and main bathroom) are 7.87 feet high. Rather than viewing these compact dimensions as a hindrance, though, the architect uses them as an opportunity to create a number of multifunctional spaces.

Casa Valls

Year: 2003 • Location: Santa Perpètua de Mogoda (Barcelona), Spain • Floor area: 851.11 square feet • Architect: Rob Dubois/Rob Dubois — Arquitecte • Photographer: Jovan Horvath

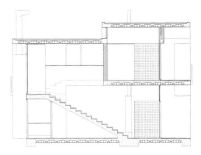

Can you describe briefly the design concept behind the project and the reason for its compactness?

The main concept of the house is to create the sensation of openness and spaces interrelated to each other, and to interpret the "raumplan'" concept of three, instead of two-dimensional spaces (a modest tribute to Adolf Loos) without falling into highly complicated shapes or structures. All features are based on quite simple geometrical shapes that are not too difficult to realize. The reason for its compactness is rather prosaic: on one hand, the limited budget, and on the other hand, the architect's desire to squeeze the most out of the space, which basically means using every square foot twice.

What is the most striking feature/element of this project that you believe makes it unique from other small-scale houses?

A well-trained architect who dedicates sufficient time to the problem will come to interesting solutions. The desperate need of most architects nowadays to achieve uniqueness results too often in sterile exercises of aesthetic, parallel to the doctor who said, "Operation successful; patient dead."

The house is reminiscent of the heroic era of modern architecture, one of the building expositions (Siedlung) of the early thirties in Vienna, where Adolf Loos and Gerrit Rietveld experimented with different solutions for tiny and "spacious" row houses. This house expresses a nostalgia for that time when architects, a bit naïvely, believed in upgrading living conditions by means of their designs.

If you were to lay down Five Commandments for effective compact architectural design, what would these be? Relate also how each commandment is fulfilled in the project.

1) Reduce the transport area (corridors) to the minimum—if this is unavoidable, overlap them as much as possible. Every square foot won is worth gold.
2) Create the longest sightlines possible to give the sensation of spaciousness and avoid the claustrophobic feeling.
3) Although compact is more or less synonymous to small, introduce "big" elements, such as double-height spaces or other elements to divert attention away from the reduced overall dimensions and toward the well-designed, eyecatching elements, as seen in this project. Create a "confusing" scale, which has always been a fun and effective game, as Robert Venturi showed us some forty years ago.
4) Have a limited budget and a small site, which helps a lot.
5) Create an ambience that evokes repose and quietness, which implicates a sober design language and a limited range of materials, colors, and textures.

The house is reminiscent of the heroic era of modern architecture.

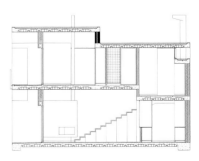

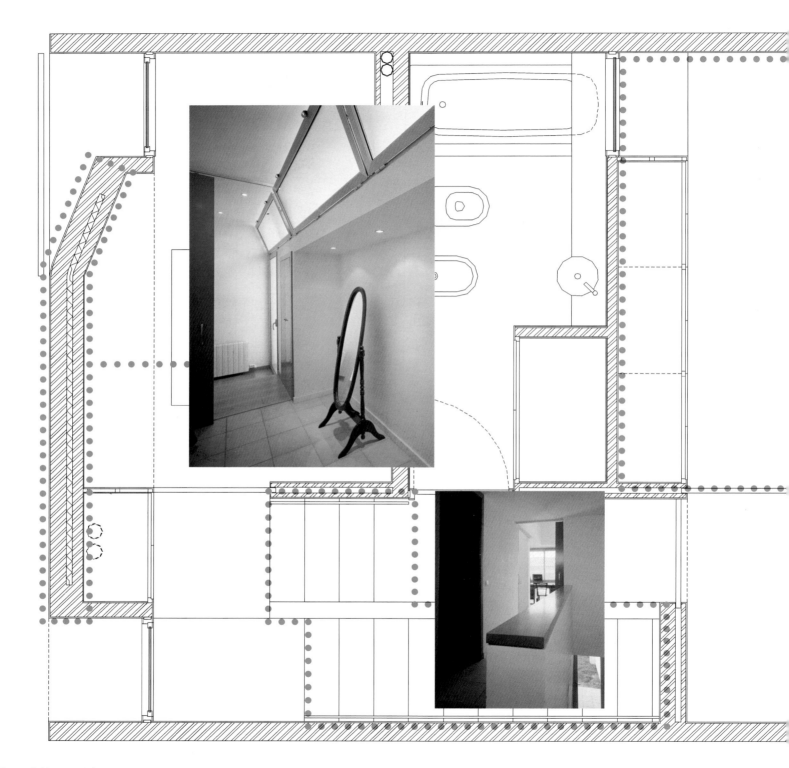

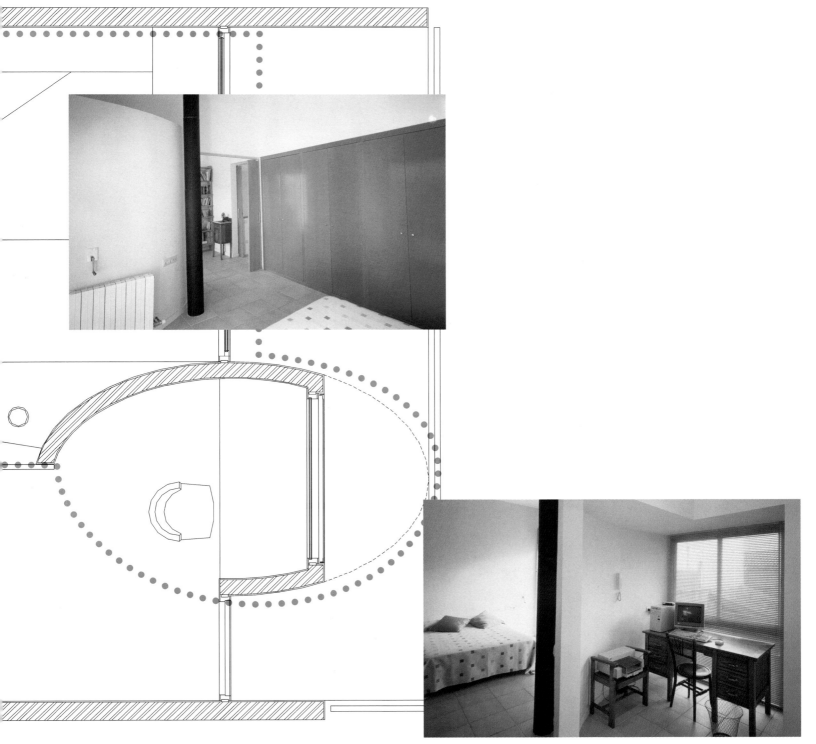

This summer house is one of a series of three residences situated on a group of islands in the Baltic Sea just north of Stockholm, Sweden. The house is 131.24 feet from the sea and found in a small pine forest.

The client wished to live in a small, compact house, yet posed a number of requirements. The constraints of the site and the budget dictated the size of the area and made the project more interesting by constantly posing the question of how a small building can be experienced in a large sense. The resulting house embodies an experimental and radical architecture that reveals the flexibility of this compact structure.

Summer House Åland

Year: 2002 • Location: Åland, Finland • Floor Area: 451.92 square feet •
Architects: Todd Saunders, Tommie Wilhelmsen/Saunders Arkitektur, Bergen & Wilhelmsen Arkitektur, Stavanger

Can you describe briefly the design concept behind the project and the reason for its compactness?

We conceived of the house as a long, continuous, and folded timber structure that you can move up, down, over, and under through various spaces. An architectural landscape forms all of the elements of the house: walls, floor, roof, and terrace. The rooms are formed through their many functions and can be used together as one space or separately by the use of glass sliding doors.

The house can be opened from the outside room between the kitchen and the bedroom to create one large room. At this level, one looks through the pine forest, but on the top of the roof one gets a fantastic view over the many islands around Åland.

What is the most striking feature/element of this project that you believe makes it unique from other small-scale houses?

One of the most striking aspects of this house is that every inch is utilized. There is absolutely no wasted space, and the space that is created either has two- or three-fold functions. One can eat breakfast on the terrace under the morning sun; or twenty people can sit and watch the evening sun by the front of the cabin, eat dinner outside on the floor between the bedroom and the "all room," and open all the glass doors to form one space for larger groups of people. Even though we describe situations that pertain to the flexibility of this small structure, the idea was not only to create a space we ourselves had little control over, but also to invite the people to use the space as freely and creatively as they could imagine. A house without borders is in many ways endless and, therefore, never compact in the negative sense of the word.

The second unique aspect of this house is that we strived to make an environmentally responsible house. The house is insulated with woven linseed fibers, and the entire wooden structure is protected with cold-pressed linseed oil. All materials come from a local sawmill. The house itself is built upon pillars so that the natural landscape and the roots of all of the trees are conserved.

If you were to lay down Five Commandments for effective compact architectural design, what would these be? Relate also how each commandment is fulfilled in the project.

1) Think of volume.
2) Connect surfaces.
3) Equate architecture with furniture (the front section of the house can be used as a long bench).
4) Think of how all of the surfaces can be utilized (the flat roof of this house is used as a roof terrace).
5) Erase hallways from plans, as they are often signs of wasted space.

A house without borders is in many ways endless.

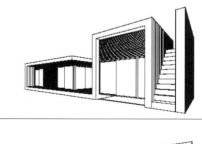

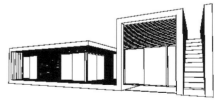

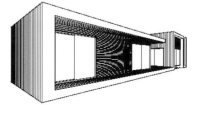

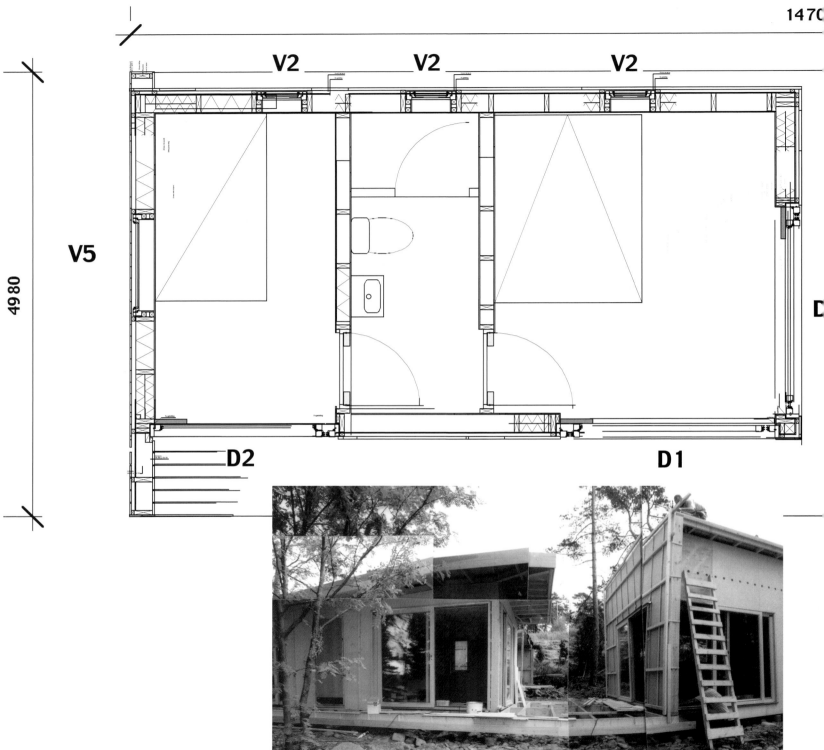

1470

V2　　　　V2　　　　V2

V5

4980

D2　　　　　　　　　　D1

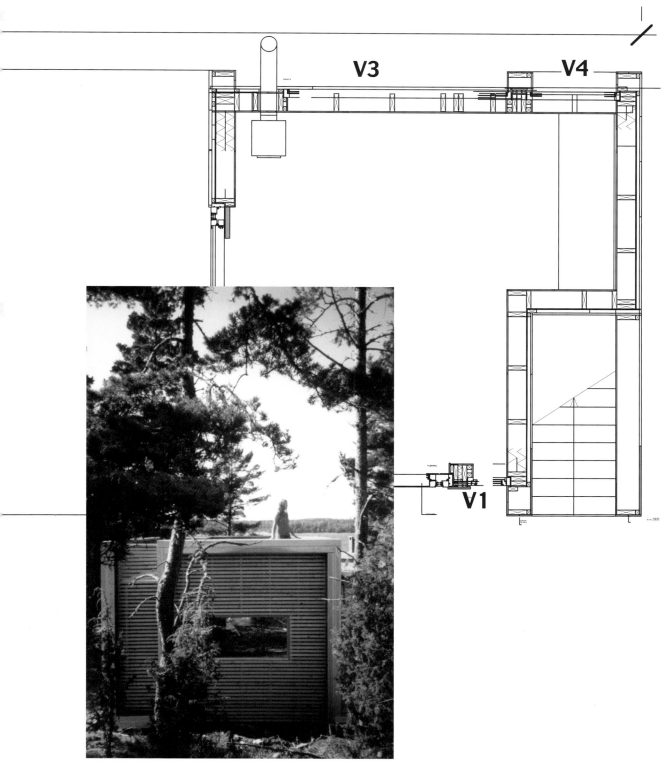

V3

V4

V1

This small-scale house has special functions as an urban-style second house. The owner planned to use this compact house for his business base in the urban core of Tokyo, in addition to his main house in the suburbs. The meeting space on the first floor is not just for the owner's private use; it is also rented out. Therefore, the approach through the entrance needed to be as open and as bright as possible, even though this space faces a narrow alley in the residential block. Each of the floors has its own function: as meeting room, office space, and living quarters, respectively. The stairway, which projects toward the road, connects these spaces, creating the visual illusion of open space throughout the house.

P·O·M Ebisu

Year: 2001 • Location: Tokyo, Japan • Floor Area: 1,258.92 square feet • Architects: Rikuo Nishimori, Hideo Kumaki/NAA • Photographer: Aki Furudate

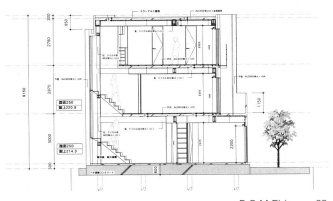

Can you describe briefly the design concept behind the project and the reason for its compactness?

If we design a floor plan for the irregularly shaped land area using simple oblong shapes, it is difficult to utilize the narrow area effectively. To solve this problem, we divided the area into two triangles, with three walls in a diagonal line from front to back, creating bigger and smaller spaces side by side. Because of the juxtaposition of the wide space and narrow spaces, the rooms appear to be bigger than they actually are. The other triangular space at the rear side of this area could have been a narrow and badly ventilated dead space. However, since it was planned in such a way so that people can see the back space through the entrance and the meeting room from the outside, it succeeds in creating an open feeling and the impression of looking bigger than its actual size. Although the stairway is also located in the minimum space, it opens widely with the glass facing the road to create the feeling of extending the space and alleviating the narrowness.

What is the most striking feature/element of this project that you believe makes it unique from other small-scale houses?

The most remarkable element is that, in addition to the living space, this house embodies two more functions in this extraordinarily small area. As a result, unnecessary elements were minimized in this building. Moreover, since the big and small spaces alternate, the house provides the illusion that the big spaces look bigger and the small ones look smaller than their actual sizes.

If you were to lay down Five Commandments for effective compact architectural design, what would these be? Relate also how each commandment is fulfilled in the project.

1) Visually create a feeling of open space. In this project, the relationship was between the width and the depth; keeping enough height in the ceiling integrated the higher and lower spaces.
2) Be flexible in the method of space configuration.
3) Utilize the relationship with the outside to the maximum.
4) Pay attention to the size of the details—a few inches difference provides a different impression in a small space.
5) Eliminate the common and redundant elements; make the plan as simple as possible.

The house provides the illusion that the big spaces look bigger and the small ones look smaller than their actual sizes.

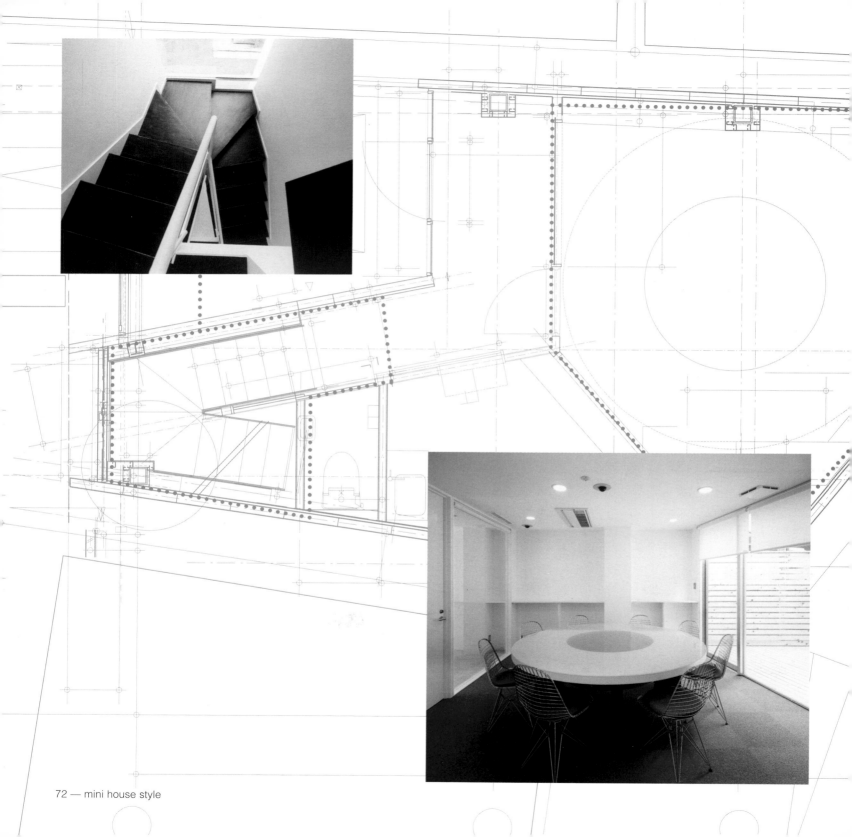

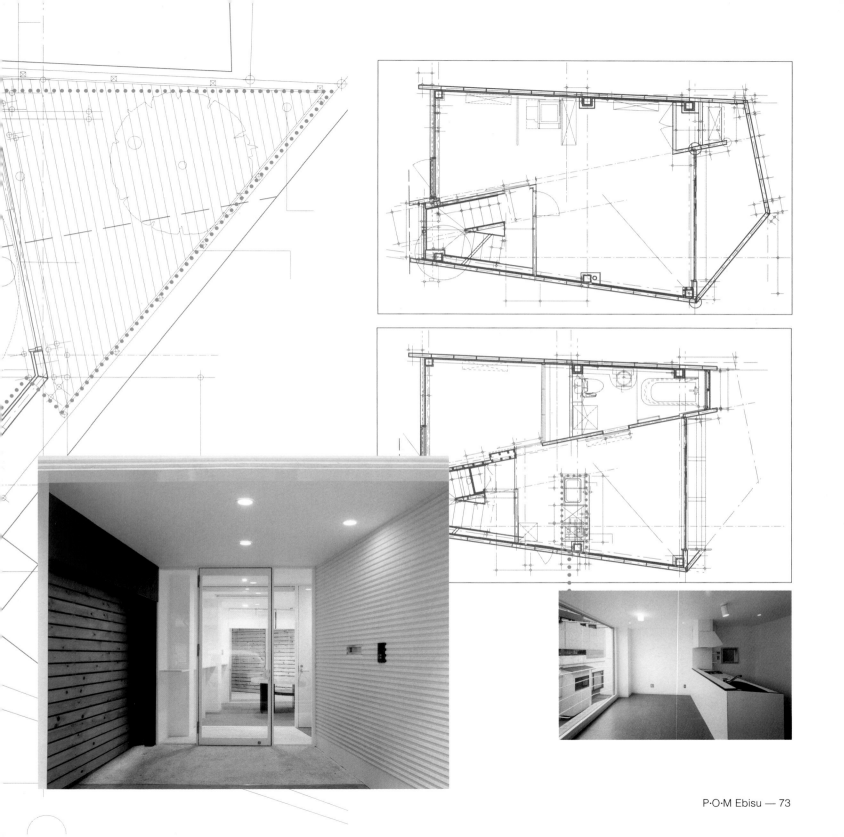

Situated in a small woodland clearing on the edge of the village of Sevgein, this house fits like a wedge between a mountainside and the end of a chain of hills, forming a gentle transition between the two. From this position, it affords a view right across the wide valley of the Upper Rhine.

Wohnhaus Willimann-Lötscher

Year: 1998 • Location: Sevgein, Switzerland • Floor Area: 624.08 square feet • Architects: Valentin Bearth, Andrea Deplazes, Daniel Ladner/Bearth & Deplazes Architekten AG • Photographer: Ralph Feiner

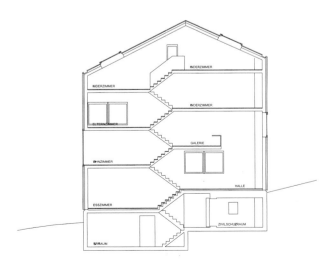

Can you describe briefly the design concept behind the project and the reason for its compactness?

The client, a family of four, requested a house with a lot of different rooms—a kind of "labyrinthine mousehole." The result is a towerlike arrangement of rooms offset at each half-storey, following the slope of the land. The entrance to the house opens into a two-storey hallway, with steps leading down to the dining room and kitchen and up to a living room with a gallery. Four more rooms are on the upper storeys.

The house's timber frame was prefabricated in sections, and the standard windows used for pitched roofs were prefitted on both façades and the roof. The client did much of the finishing work, like timber cladding and paintwork, himself.

What is the most striking feature/element of this project that you believe makes it unique from other small-scale houses?

The two rooms on each floor are arranged along the shared long wall in such a way as to create a vertical spiral of space within the house, or a kind of "inner topography." This has the effect of maximizing the interior volume despite the small size of the individual rooms.

The rooms create a kind of "inner topography."

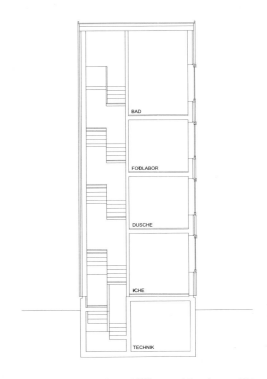

If you were to lay down Five Commandments for effective compact architectural design, what would these be? Relate also how each commandment is fulfilled in the project.

1) Form a transition between the structure and the natural surroundings.
2) Use vertical spaces.
3) Use manual labor as much as possible.
4) Be inventive with the use of materials.
5) Use multiple levels.

Wohnhaus Willimann-Lötscher — 79

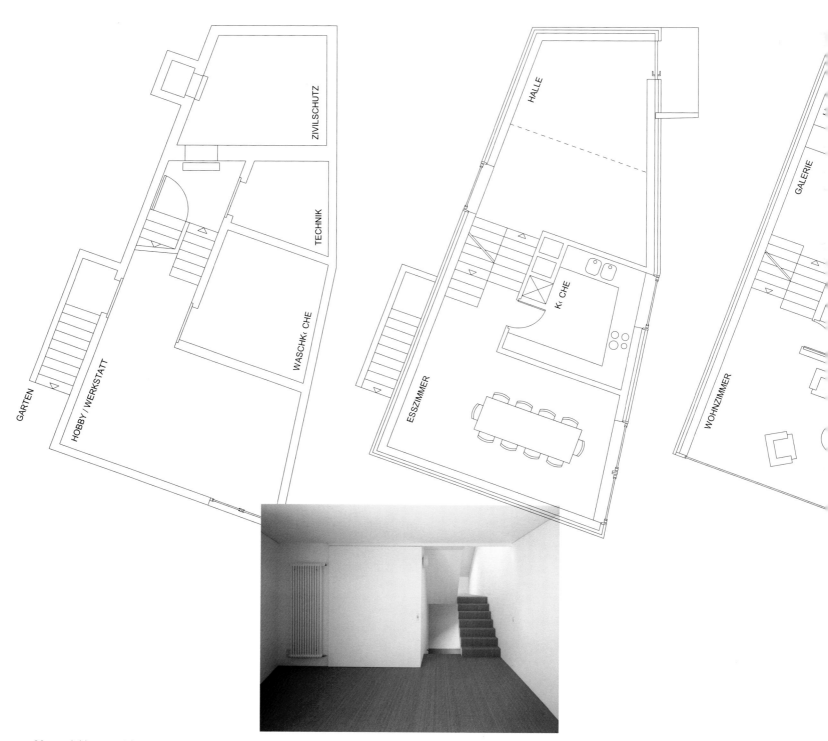

ZIVILSCHUTZ

TECHNIK

WASCHKÜCHE

HOBBY / WERKSTATT

GARTEN

HALLE

KÜCHE

ESSZIMMER

GALERIE

WOHNZIMMER

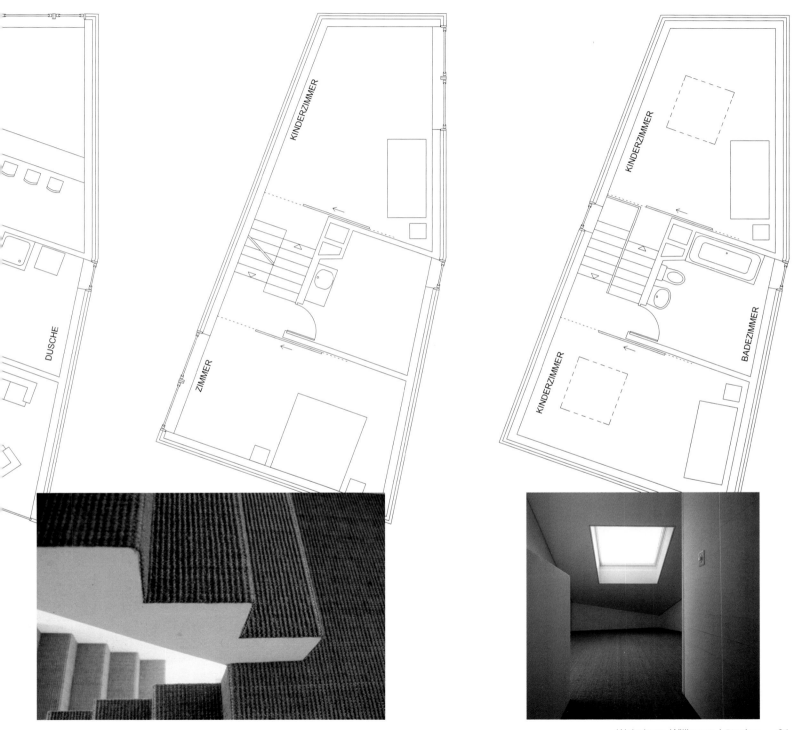

KINDERZIMMER

ZIMMER

DUSCHE

KINDERZIMMER

KINDERZIMMER

BADEZIMMER

Drawing its inspiration from early California modernism, the Fineman Residence celebrates the simplicity of a floating glass house. It continues the ongoing research at Lorcan O'Herlihy Architects into new materials and methods of fabrication allowing the rediscovery of the relationship between material and design. The existing structure was redesigned to carry the continuity of the overall idea of a house fragmented into different pieces.

Fineman Residence

Year Established: 2003 • Location: Los Angeles, California, USA • Floor Area: 1,589ft² (147 m²) • Architects: Lorcan O'Herlihy, David Thompson, Mariana Boctor, Jeffrey Chan, Juan Diego Gerscovich, Franka Diehnelt/Lorcan O'Herlihy Architects • Photographer: Michael Weschler

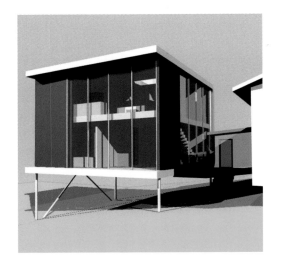

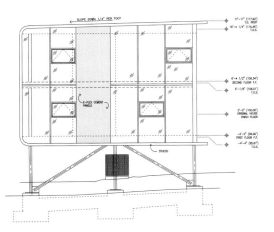

Can you describe briefly the design concept behind the project and the reason for its compactness?

A portion of the existing house was carved away detaching the garage and creating an outdoor courtyard of the new public areas of the house. Outdoor rooms were created through the use of the negative space framed by the building volumes. The rear structure, inspired by the eucalyptus trees in the rear, floats above the ground to embrace the experience of living in an abstract tree house. This proposal creates a new platform, elevated in space.

What is the most striking feature/element of this project that you believe makes it unique from other small-scale houses?

The structure forms a "C" shaped object by folding upward into a supporting wall which in turn bends over to become the roof. To enclose this shape a panelized system of glass and cement board gently undulates to create an elegant rhythm that houses the sleeping quarters of the residence.

If you were to lay down Five Commandments for effective compact architectural design, what would these be? Relate also how each commandment is fulfilled in the project.

1) Establish efficiency and compactness in organization and materials.
2) Use the element of transparency—glass walls and an open plan make the space feel expansive.
3) Use multi-functional spaces—the bridge acts as a library sitting area; thick walls are used to absorb functions such as the storage and laundry room instead of providing distinct rooms for each.
4) Attain mobility—the simple act of moving a slider is able to drastically reorganize spaces; minimal means maximum effect.
5) Create a difference in repetition—interrupt a backdrop of repetition to create unique instances, spaces, details and junctions.

Outdoor rooms were created through the use of negative space.

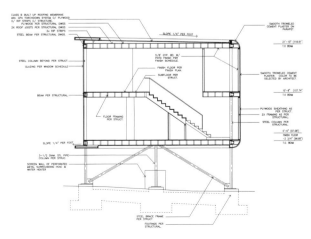

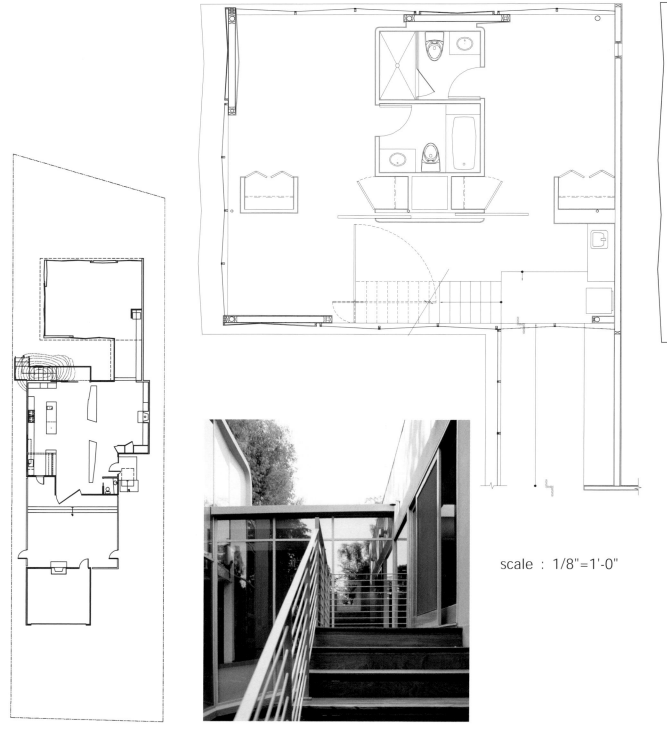

scale : 1/8"=1'-0"

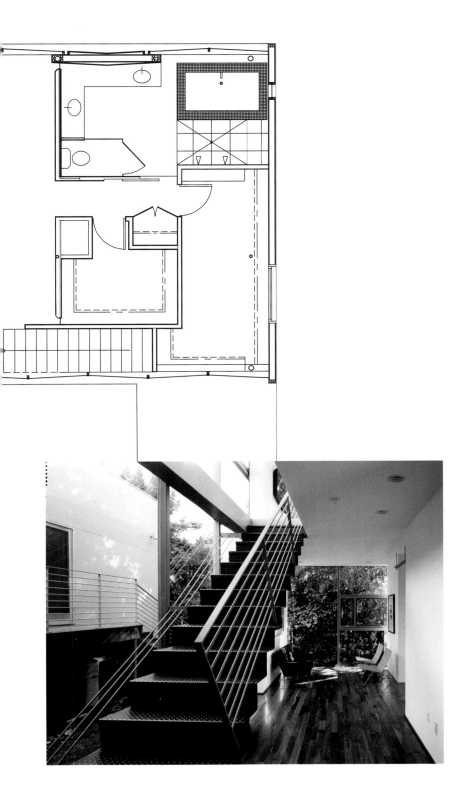

Three dwellings were required on a site occupied by an old storage shed of poor construction. The new houses developed into three tubes of space that were consistent in their dimensions and details; inserted into these three tubes are the internal walls and first floors. Within this context, the internal finishes and layouts are adapted and "tuned" to the requirements of each of the occupants.

During the design process, the architects deliberately sought to push the development of each internal space in a clearly different direction to experiment with the idea of three identical spaces being treated in distinct ways. The perception of space, acoustics, and materials provides a concrete demonstration of how subtle changes to these elements can radically remake that space.

Three Houses Rathmines

Year: 1999 • Location: Dublin, Ireland • Floor Area: 1,076 square feet each house • Architects: Dermot Boyd/Boyd Cody Architects, Paul Kelly/FKL Architects • Photographer: Cillian Hayes

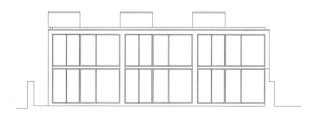

Can you describe briefly the design concept behind the project and the reason for its compactness?

The first house employs a palate of natural materials: stone on the ground floor, timber upstairs, and the bathroom lined in glazed mosaic. One kitchen is suspended, and the other is grounded on the floor. All the fixed furniture elements on the first floor are parallel to the longitudinal axis of the space, maintaining a spatial flow from one end of the house to the other.

The second house consists of white floors, walls, and ceiling, which unify the space and emphasize the concept of the tube. On the first floor, the kitchen, stairs, and storage occupy the dimensions set up by the solid panels in the façade. The stairs fold up and under the floating block of the stainless steel kitchen. The fixed storage unit relates to the stairs through its dimension and position. On the ground floor, colored fluorescent tubes and mirrors set up a variety of surprising relationships between the bathroom and the door to the entrance hall.

The third house uses color and material to allow for maximum flexibility within the space. In the entry, visitors are drawn upwards by an open stair toward the first-floor roof light, which allows light into the depth of the plan and is maximized to provide an unrestricted view to the sky. The rubber floor in the hall matches the color of the carpet on the stairs, reducing the visual disruption inherent in using a number of materials in a small space.

Subtle changes to elements can radically remake the space.

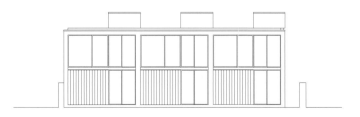

What is the most striking feature/element of this project that you believe makes it unique from other small-scale houses?

This project is unique in its treatment of three buildings with a consistent façade and spatial idea. The exteriors of the three houses are all treated in the same way, each façade detailed in a manner to make a flush, taut surface across the end of the three tubes. The materials of the elevations have a similar color tone—the silver-grey, untreated iroko blends with the window frames and the external plaster of the tubes. Within this consistent context, occupants have the liberty of treating their space to suit their interests and lifestyle.

If you were to lay down Five Commandments for effective compact architectural design, what would these be? Relate also how each commandment is fulfilled in the project.

1) Maximize the dimensions of the space in the house—we reduced the number of rooms to the minimum, eliminated unnecessary ensuite bathrooms, and inserted the utility facilities under the stairs.
2) Capture as much light as possible—we maximized the light with floor-to-ceiling windows and a central roof light in the depth of the plan.
3) Limit the number of materials to reduce the visual discord within a small house—House 1 has a stone floor across the complete ground floor, under the stairs, and under the bathroom; House 2 uses a white, cushion-backed vinyl and an iroko; House 3 uses color to unify all of the spaces in the house.
4) Make a compact form—the external materials of the houses reflect that of the rear elevations of the adjacent houses.
5) Ensure a clarity of idea and concept—floors and ceiling glass with aluminum solid panels reinforce the reading of the tube externally. The window liners, recesses for lights, and blinds are all detailed to maintain the spatial flow through the tube; the solid panels of the façade are detailed, with shadow gaps internally to disassociate these panels from the walls of the tube.

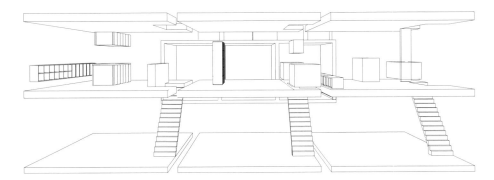

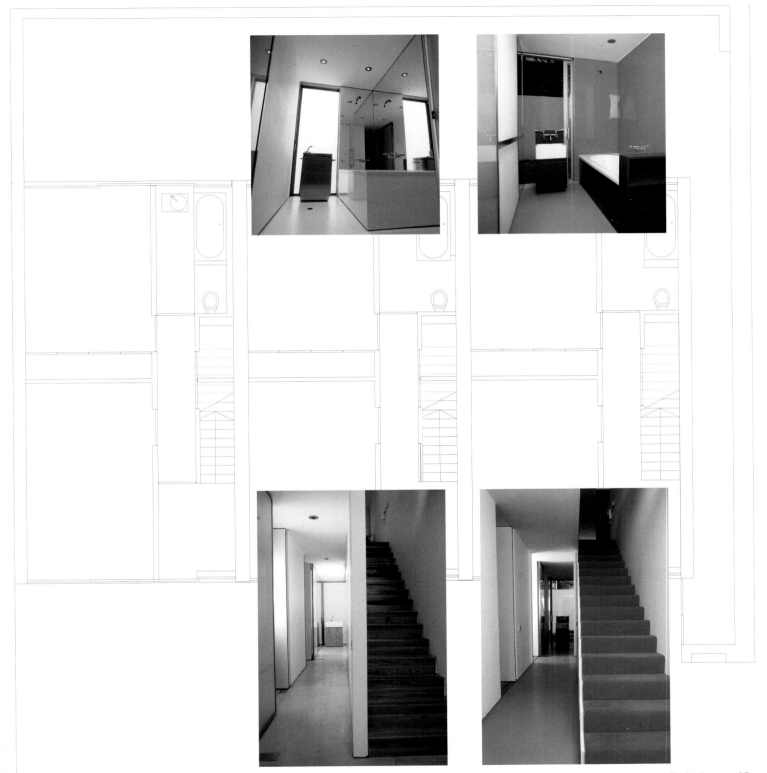

Gae House is located along the former Mekama train line, which opened in Tokyo in 1923. There has been a consistent relationship between the roadside and the greenery in this residential area throughout its eighty-year history; some blocks are still surrounded entirely by hedges. However, due to the employment of the inheritance tax, this site was sold piece by piece, and the frontage was narrowed to 19.69–26.25 feet. The hedge also had to be replaced by a parking space.

The design of the house, therefore, effectively kept the building coverage at 50 percent to suit the environment. The roof that was intended to cover the entire land area was angled to the north, facing the road, and was determined by the construction requirements. The overhang between the roof and the wall became the shelter over the parking area and made space for the hedge to continue along the boundary from the neighboring house. The resulting space highlights the ways in which a compact site can accommodate both form and function.

Gae House

Year: 2003 • Location: Tokyo, Japan • Floor Area: 951.40 square feet • Architects: Yoshiharu Tsukamoto, Momoyo Kaijima/Atelier Bow-Wow, Tsukamoto Laboratory of Toyko Institute of Technology (collaborators) • Photographers: Shinkenchiku-sha, Yoshiharu Tsukamoto

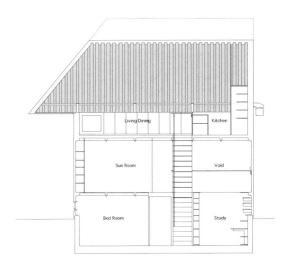

Can you describe briefly the design concept behind the project and the reason for its compactness?

All of the elements in the lot and the house are arranged to make their intended functions outstanding and effective, and to reveal not only their original purposes but also their unique roles in the building as a whole. The relationship of mutual dependence among the parts of this house creates an organic architectural experience, which we call an "elastic space."

What is the most striking feature/element of this project that you believe makes it unique from other small-scale houses?

The bedroom and husband's office space are located in the semi-basement, and the living room and kitchen are installed directly under the roof. Some non-habitable spaces are in the middle level of the house, such as the entrance and plumbing facilities. Light from the outside is reflected on the white outer wall and creates an "embracing light" that eliminates shadows in the interior. The surrounding greenery, the orangey light from the sunset, and the pedestrians' shadows on the road are reflected vaguely in this embracing light, which seems to expand or reduce each of these elements, rather than reflect them directly one by one. The discovery of this embracing feeling resulted in the concept of the "elastic space," which each element of this house consists of in its own expanded quality.

If you were to lay down Five Commandments for effective compact architectural design, what would these be? Relate also how each commandment is fulfilled in the project.

1) Maintain proportion among the windows, furniture, and rooms; and manage the direction and distance of their behavior.
2) Consider the owner's daily schedule, combine the functions of the house, and minimize the closed areas.
3) Situate the entrance at the center of the traffic line.
4) Use the surrounding scenery from the window as a part of the plan.
5) Make an effort to use areas with spaces outside, such as the gap between houses.

An "embracing light" eliminates shadows in the interior.

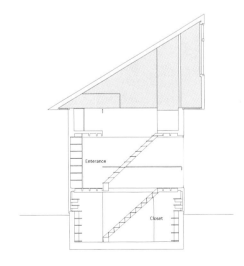

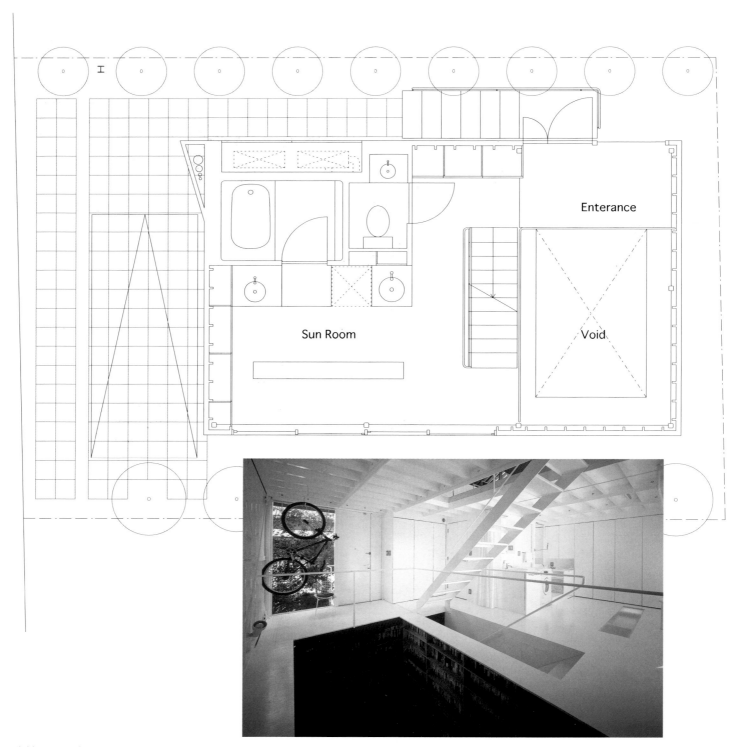

Enterance

Sun Room

Void

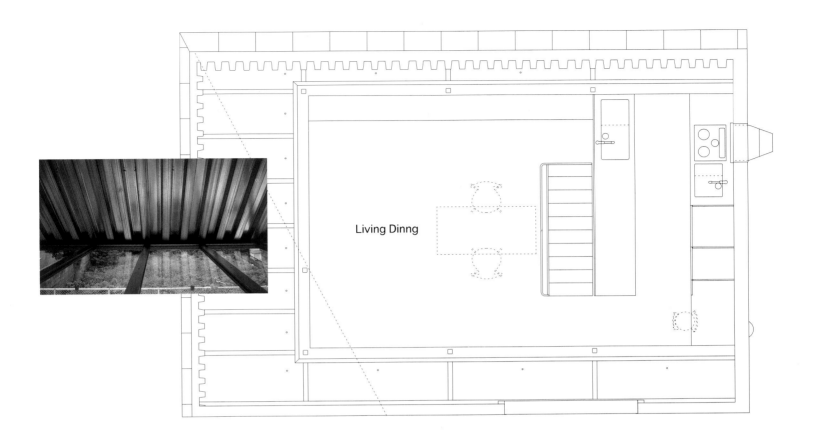

Living Dinng

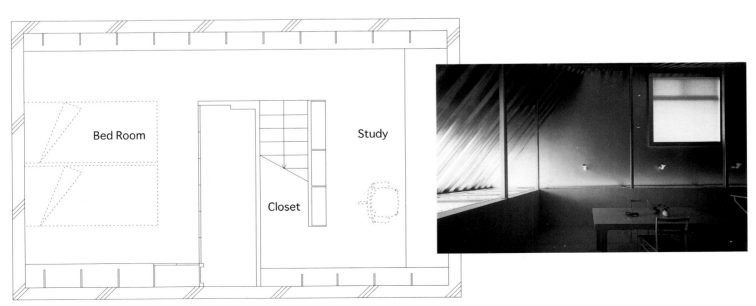

Bed Room

Study

Closet

This villa is located in a narrow strip of woodland between open fields and a lake. The black oil finish of the timber buildings echoes the dark tone of the pine forest's edge. The building opens toward the lake and is almost totally enclosed in the direction of the fields.

The narrow interior space continues outward into the yard. The foliage of the birch trees shades the interior from scorching sunlight in the summer. The villa's close relationship to the landscape allows the outside environment to become a part of the inner space, making the spaces appear bigger than they are.

Villa Linnanmäki

Year: 2002 • Location: Somero, Finland • Floor Area: 1,194.36 square-foot villa, 279.76 square-foot terrace • Architects: Risto Huttunen, Santeri Lipasti/Arkkitehtisuunnittelu Huttunen & Lipasti • Photographer: Marko Huttunen

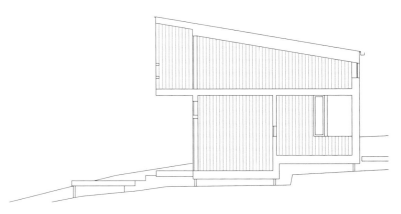

Can you describe briefly the design concept behind the project and the reason for its compactness?
The villa is designed for a family of four. It is used for vacations throughout the year. When the kids are older, the parents plan to move there permanently. The building was originally supposed to be much smaller, but the idea of using it as a home made a bigger design necessary.

The design concept for the villa came from the surrounding landscape and the desire to leave the site in its natural state. The buildings were sited along a pathway that winds between birch trees. The path begins at the edge of the field and runs through the villa, by the sauna, and to the lakeshore.

With a few simple moves, a number of spaces with different characters were created: the villa opens only toward the lake; the roof slopes in two directions; the floor is terraced in two levels; and the masonry wall divides the central space.

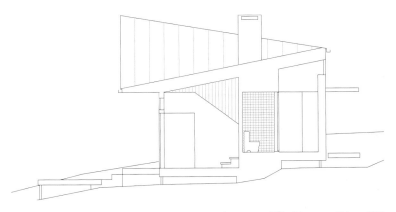

What is the most striking feature/element of this project that you believe makes it unique from other small-scale houses?

The slopes of the roof give the building a very strong character on the outside and organize the inner spaces. For example, the first floor is occupied by the kids. The height of the room varies from 2.62 feet up to 6.89 feet, so the space is good for sleeping on one end and high enough for adults on the other end. In the middle of the two, it is just the right size for kids to play in.

The other striking element is that the whole wall facing the lake is made of glass. Otherwise, the building is almost totally enclosed to the landscape. Because of the glass wall, even the narrow spaces feel big, and the yard full of birch trees becomes a part of the inner spaces.

If you were to lay down Five Commandments for effective compact architectural design, what would these be? Relate also how each commandment is fulfilled in the project.

1) Use the landscape.
2) Think ecologically.
3) Make it simple.
4) Make it functional.
5) Use the right materials.

The design concept for the villa came from the surrounding landscape.

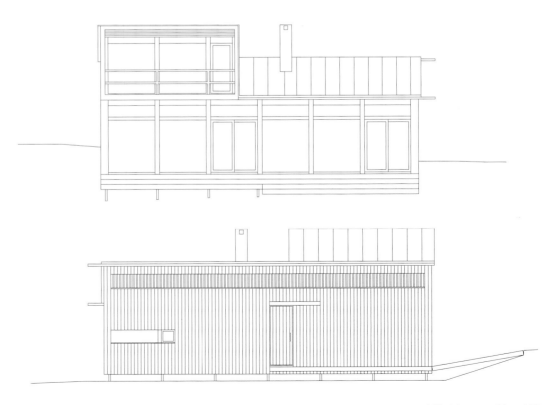

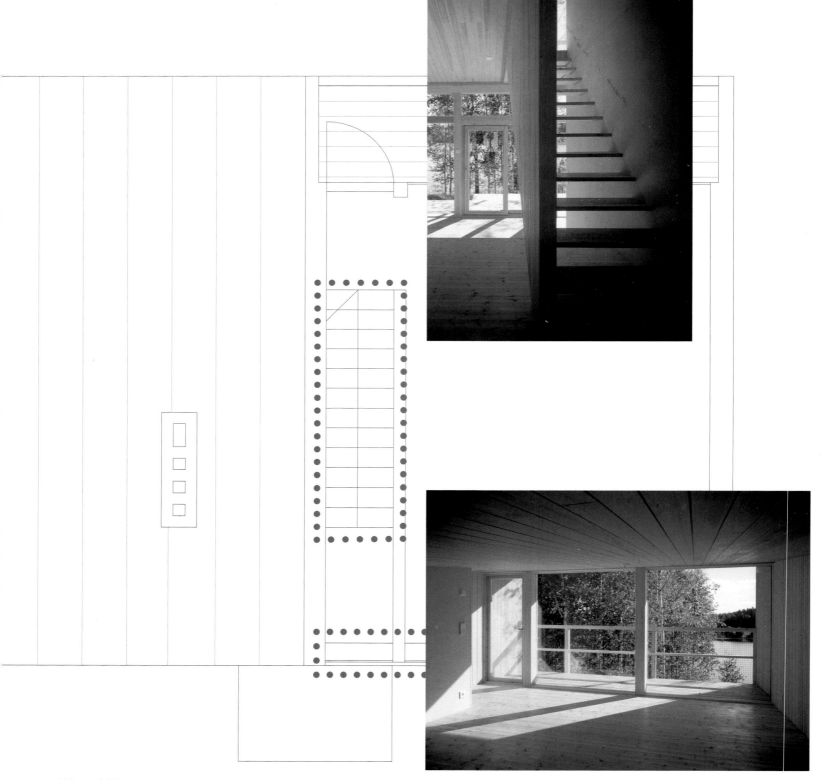

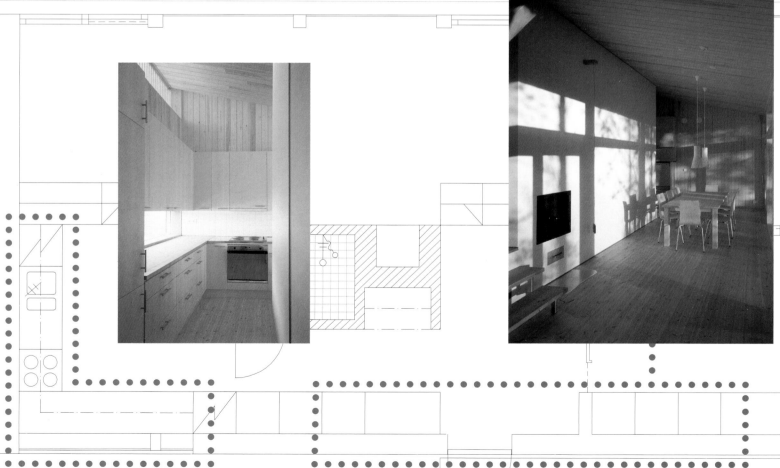

This holiday house represents the tradition of an another home detached from everyday life and placed in a natural setting. It is situated 984.30 feet from the coastline, but it lies in a suburbanlike environment that consists of a traditional grid plan with equally sized square plots. As in the suburbs, the surrounding houses are very similar in both function and style and are exact copies of normal, single-family dwellings, only in miniature form.

The project exploits the possibilities of making new architectural experiences within well-known architectural forms. The strict and conservative building codes for the area and a strong wish to make the architecture oppose the suburbanlike surroundings provoked an idea to radically blend nature and traditional architectural forms.

Summer House in Dyngby

Year: 1999 • Location: Dyngby, Denmark • Floor Area: 936.12 square feet • Architects: Claus Hermansen, Jonas Qvesel/Claus Hermansen Architects • Photographers: Anders Kavin, Poul Ib Henriksen

Can you describe briefly the design concept behind the project and the reason for its compactness?

The brief called for a house with a maximum floor area of 968.40 square feet, according to building regulations. The house would be used as a meeting place for parents, adult children, and friends, so it required several separated areas that offer both privacy and room for many people to gather. To enhance the feeling of different domains within the house, space is organized around a central entrance that divides the house into private and "public" areas. The twisted angles in the layout are a pragmatic way to connect many rooms with a minimum of corridor space: seven doors connect via a 43.04 square-foot corridor that integrates the entrance with the technical and laundry facilities.

What is the most striking feature/element of this project that you believe makes it unique from other small-scale houses?

The radical way of living with nature is used to create a precise Euclidian geometry.

If you were to lay down Five Commandments for effective compact architectural design, what would these be? Relate also how each commandment is fulfilled in the project.

1) Think pragmatically—the house is really "a machine for living in," more than a representational space. Due to the small floor area, the house had to be organized to ensure that life would be comfortable.

2) Don't think of the plan as a perfect, purified geometry. The liberation from the "elegant" plan gave richness to a special diversity and enhanced the special character of the different domains.

3) Think in three dimensions. The third dimension gives an opportunity to enhance special drama in a small area. The organization of the house is equally related to the volume and the floor area.

4) Be inventive. A critical approach to common solutions can be tested in small-scale projects, and elements can be combined in new ways; the space between the metal panels and the outside cladding on the east façade is enlarged and used for storing gardening tools.

5) Use daily life basics as fuel for architectural invention. The inhabitants' behavior and their peculiarities are the rituals to celebrate in single housing projects. The clients' wish for a large open assembly space and private study rooms became the two special opponents that created the tension in the special concept.

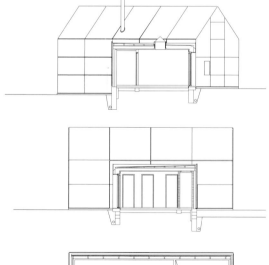

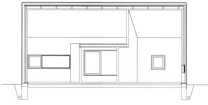

The third dimension gives an opportunity to enhance special drama in a small area.

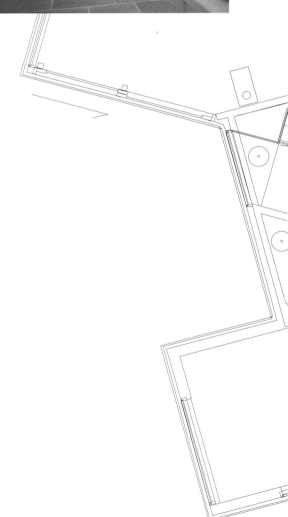

This project aimed to bring out the latent possibilities of a northern slope, which had been neglected as a residential area, and to transform it into an attractive space. This slope is located on a hill to the north of a new housing estate. The owner wished to have a house for himself, his wife, and his two children in a district with convenient utilities near his office. This site was chosen for its location in a natural forest on a hill 321.10 feet above sea level, with a view of the Seto Inland Sea to the east and the Chugoku Mountains to the north; the price was less than half of the other lots in this area because it was a leftover tract on the northern slope.

With regards to the space configuration, an artificial foundation was raised on the northern slope to provide living space in the semi-basement underneath it. In summer, this foundation shuts out the strong sunshine, and a cool air stream circulates from the bottom to the top of the slope. When there is a lull in the wind, which is characteristic near the Seto Inland Sea, the chimney becomes effective for air circulation. In winter, the sunshine streams down all day along the slope, and the space beneath the artificial foundation becomes a green, winter garden. Furthermore, this space is surrounded by a consistent environment throughout the year because of the small wall area that is exposed to the air outside.

Sloping North House

Year: 2003 • Location: Yamaguchi, Japan • Floor Area: 1,112.58 square feet •
Architect: Hiroshi Sambuichi/Sambuichi Architects • Photographers: Hiroshi Sambuichi, Shinkenchiku-sha

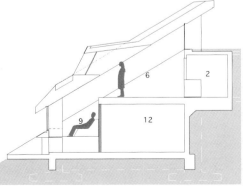

Can you describe briefly the design concept behind the project and the reason for its compactness?

The building itself has the flexibility to cope with all the natural environmental considerations and a form led by natural energy that does not depend on energy conservation products, such as solar panels or ecology products developed by other industries.

In accordance with the conditions of light, air, heat, wind, and the shape of the slope, the angle of the roof was set at 11:18. There is a large aperture in the center of the roof toward the north that gives a view of the mountains. It was not necessary to install blinds to provide shade. Life is enriched by the bounties of nature from north to south. The total cost was cut by minimizing the land price and by trial recycling of concrete molds. There are also various levels on the slope. The house was planned to have a more private atmosphere towards the lower levels, while gently increasing the visual axis and atmosphere on the upper levels. The space has a rich feeling of nature and family life, as the owner required.

What is the most striking feature/element of this project that you believe makes it unique from other small-scale houses?

The house creates a new concept of values for things that are neglected and undervalued. These values relate to "living toward the north" and being attuned to the flexible responses of various factors, such as the sunshine on the north slope, heat, climate, natural environment, sight, and economical efficiency.

If you were to lay down Five Commandments for effective compact architectural design, what would these be? Relate also how each commandment is fulfilled in the project.

1) Provide the owner with a comfortable life.
2) Combine boldness and modesty.
3) Work on the project with a comprehensible configuration and theme.
4) Bring out the full potential of the material.
5) Be closely linked with the landscape, climate, vegetation, and hydraulics.

The house creates a new concept of values for things that are neglected and undervalued.

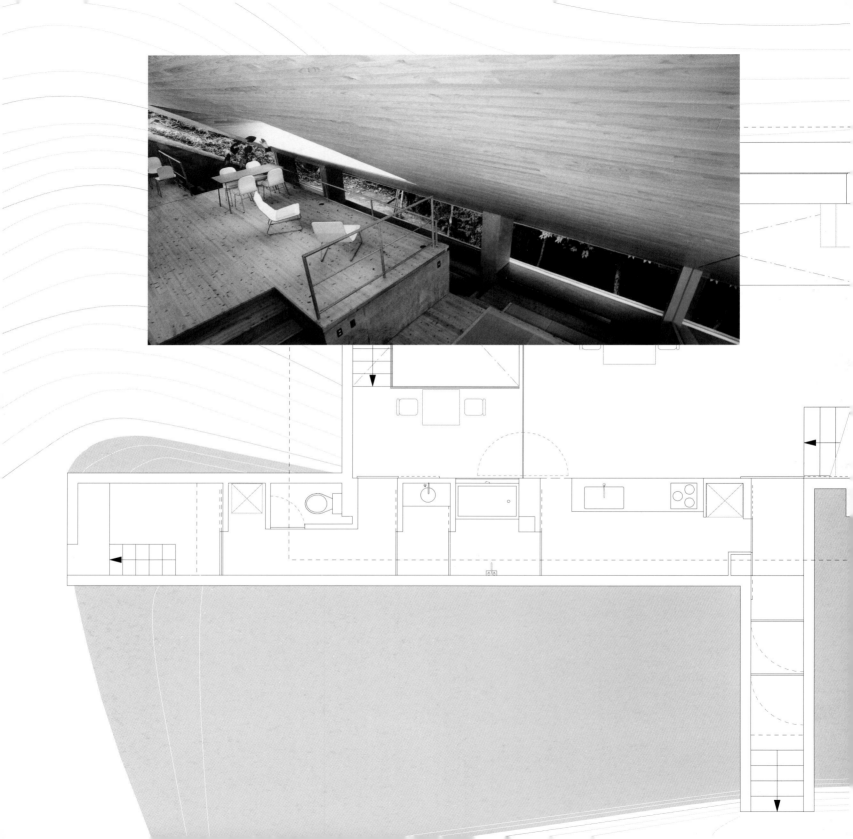

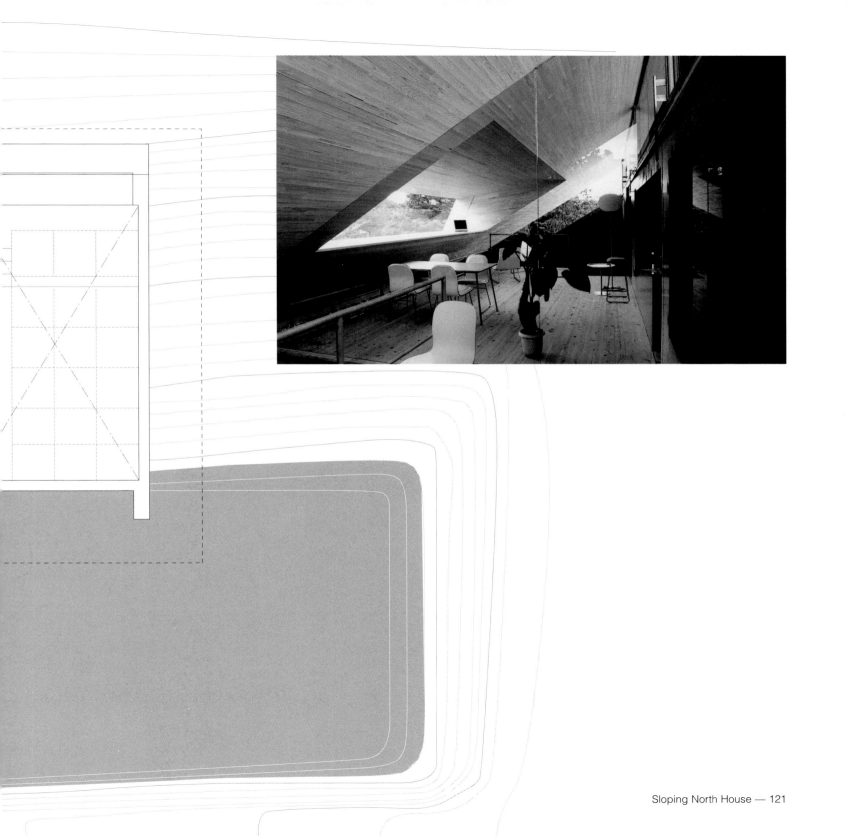

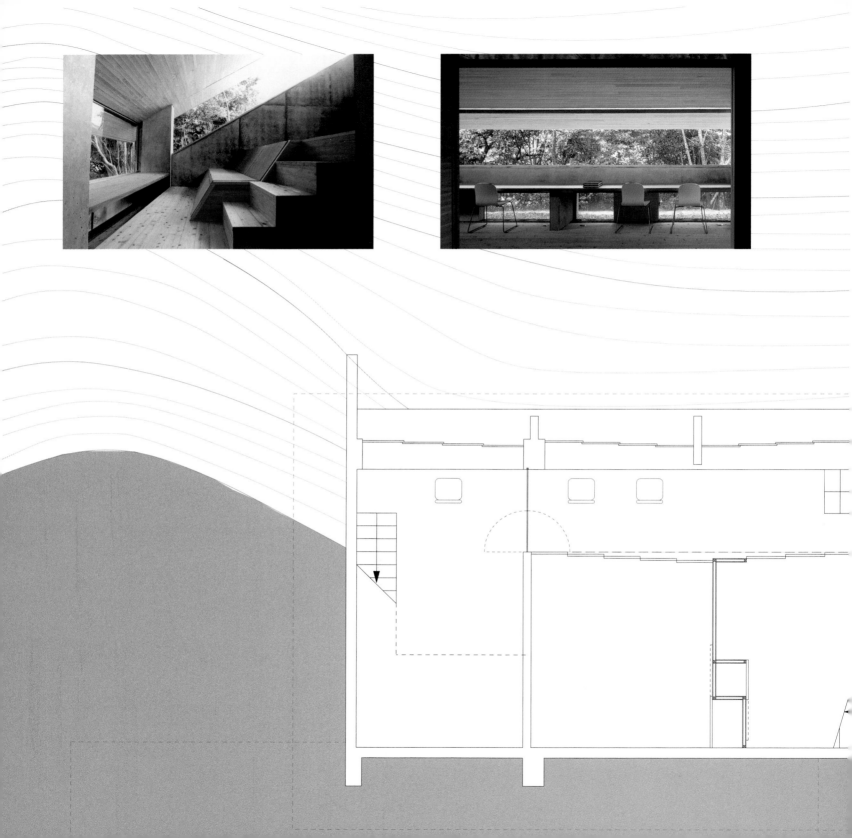

Intended as a follow-up to the firm's design work undertaken for the "36 Proposals for a Home" project, the scheme for MR House illustrates the architects' ambition to make an architect-designed house for the same price as a basic Wates home, while ensuring that it meshes subtly with its surroundings.

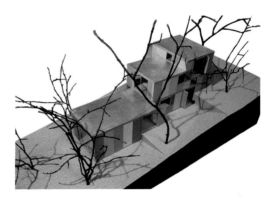

MR House

Year: 2000 • Location: Pompone, France • Floor Area: 1,506 square feet •
Architects: Emmanuelle Marin-Trottin, David Trottin/Marin + Trottin Périphériques Architectes •
Photographers: H. Abadie, L. Boegly

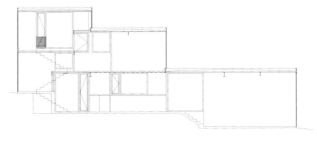

Can you describe briefly the design concept behind the project and the reason for its compactness?

The tightly narrow plot of 55.78 feet gave rise to an elongated design, which has the advantage of reducing the building's visual impact on the garden. By the same token, this strip form creates a historical link with the farming activity that used to take place on the site. The rooms unfold along the slope, from the living room to the bedroom. Both public and private spaces are conceived as half-storys so as to be in close contact with the garden at all times.

Both public and private spaces are conceived as half-storeys.

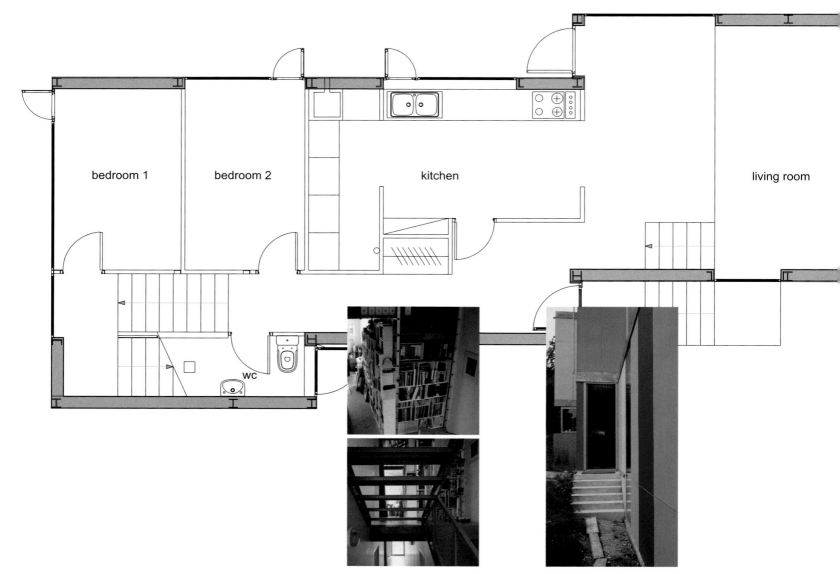

bedroom 1

bedroom 2

kitchen

living room

WC

What is the most striking feature/element of this project that you believe makes it unique from other small-scale houses?

Stretched along a strip of marshy land in the Seine and Marne regions of France, this metal-framed house seems to form part of the landscape. The dwelling slopes with the 15 percent drop of the land and is camouflaged by greenery, while the painted panels of the façade blend with the gardenlike chromatic pixels. Huge windows frame the lower and upper gardens. As a final touch, small shutters let in the fragrance of the elements, thus highlighting the relationship between interior and exterior.

If you were to lay down Five Commandments for effective compact architectural design, what would these be? Relate also how each commandment is fulfilled in the project.

1) Economy!
2) Economy!
3) Economy!
4) Economy!
5) Economy!

bedroom 3

gap up to the bedroom 1   bathroom   office

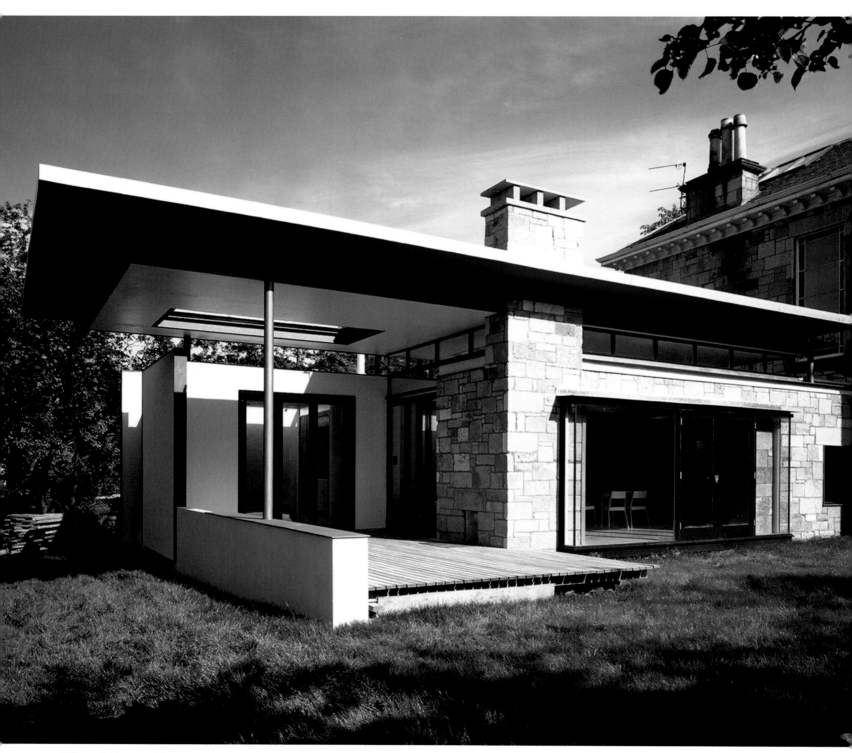

This project's scope comprises a substantial remodeling of the rear of an existing 19th century stone mansion in the south of Glasgow. In addition to the kitchen and utility spaces, the plan accommodates living areas, a study, and a covered terrace orientated toward a private garden that faces the west and south. Key alterations on the ground floor enliven the existing rooms and enhance their relationship with the new work added to the rear side, creating a living space where the exterior spaces are linked to the existing structure.

Waddell House

Year: 2002 · Location: Pollockshields, Glasgow, Scotland, UK · Floor Area: 860.80 square feet · Architects: Roderick Kemsley, Christopher Platt/Studio KAP · Photographer: Keith Hunter

Can you describe briefly the design concept behind the project and the reason for its compactness?

The design creates an informal and open sequence of the living, dining and kitchen, storytelling, and study areas under a new, oversailing roof that links the interior spaces with the redesigned exterior spaces. The clients desired an informal and social space to complement the more formal rooms in the existing mansion.

What is the most striking feature/element of this project that you believe makes it unique from other small-scale houses?

The project has a complex plan, carefully designed to create a number of distinct places, all in visual (and therefore social) contact with each other. Thus, living, dining, storytelling, cooking, and outdoor sitting all take place underneath a large, modern stainless steel roof.

If you were to lay down Five Commandments for effective compact architectural design, what would these be? Relate also how each commandment is fulfilled in the project.

1) Exploit the section to allow different types of daylight in and different types of views out. A new transition space is created at the same floor level as the existing house, which has two circular rooflights and a carefully positioned and sized window that offers views of the grass outside. Daylight is carefully controlled, and although there is much glass, there is never glare.

2) Create different places within one overall space to maximize different experiences of being there. The oversailing roof above the walls "floats" by separating them by glass and allowing the plan to meander in and out; floor levels and ceiling levels change as new places are established.

3) Maintain a careful attitude to detail, since small spaces are closer to details than large spaces—how openings are framed (in chunky or minimalist frames) alters the perception of the exterior from the interior.

4) Carefully consider what elements (furniture or storage) can be built-in and what can or should be freestanding—discreet locations for the toilet, utility, boiler rooms, and kitchen storage allow a certain amount of open living by hiding the space where the everyday "stuff" of a home is housed.

5) Design elements or spaces that can solve more than one problem at once—the spaces are designed to suit a young couple with a growing family or could just as easily accommodate a more self-contained arrangement for an older, parental/grandparent group.

The house creates distinct places,
all in visual and social contact with each other.

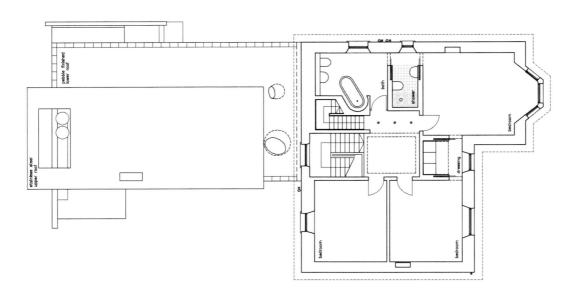

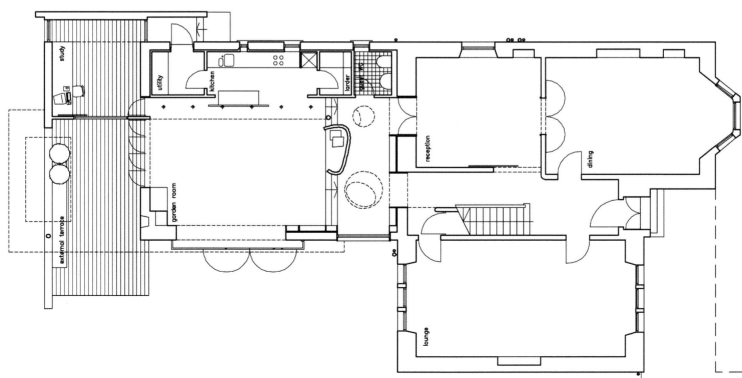

Sited on the road with virtually no setback, the Fernau/Cunniff house was originally a tiny, undistinguished, and "affordable" structure from the fifties that was built on the "carriage house" model. The wooded lot's comparatively spacious rear yard slopes quickly away from the road to a creek. The original plan had a straightforward logic and a quirky character but failed to take advantage of the site's untapped potential. The architectural impulse that guided the remodeling was the reinforcement of the urban-rural character of the house by reasserting its "roadhouse" quality and making a virtue of its location on the street. Simultaneously, the house was reoriented towards the forest, the creek, and the view to San Francisco Bay.

Fernau/Cunniff Residence

Year: 1991 • Location: Berkeley, California, USA • Floor Area: 1,500 square feet • Architects: Laura Hartman, Richard Fernau/Fernau and Hartman Architects • Photographers: Richard Barnes, Christopher Irion

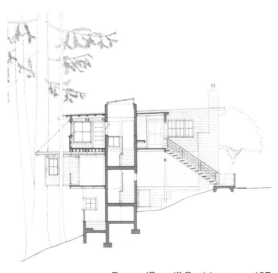

Can you describe briefly the design concept behind the project and the reason for its compactness?

The compact size of the residence was established from the beginning. The solution to the challenging site was a three-story addition, linked by a stair tower that both ventilates and brings light deep into the center of the house. A range of wood products was combined with various finishes to help differentiate the various spaces and interventions. A line of sight through the house was accomplished by cutting new openings, both interior and exterior, visually connecting the street and the trees beyond. The new bedroom and study were stacked under the den, making the link to the creek two stories below; and a sleeping porch, accessed from the bedroom through a wall that slides out from the house and hangs from its track among the trees, was suspended under a porch supported by an unpeeled redwood log. The redwood column engages the existing trees close at hand, further connecting the house to its surroundings.

What is the most striking feature/element of this project that you believe makes it unique from other small-scale houses?

By stacking and combining spaces, the Fernau/Cunniff residence makes the most of the available square footage: a deck becomes a sleeping porch; moveable walls offer a variety of different types of spaces; and mobile furniture rolls out to fit each new need. In its flexibility, the house accommodates a family of four.

If you were to lay down Five Commandments for effective compact architectural design, what would these be? Relate also how each commandment is fulfilled in the project.

1) Attain flexibility—different spaces bend around disparate uses.
2) Focus on details—refined detailing brings interest to this small scale.
3) Use high quality or unusual materials.
4) Be innovative—new ideas, like bringing the bedroom out into the porch, allow for spaces to grow.
5) Create a "push-pull" concept—as different spaces overlap, dynamism develops.

Combining spaces makes the most of the available square footage.

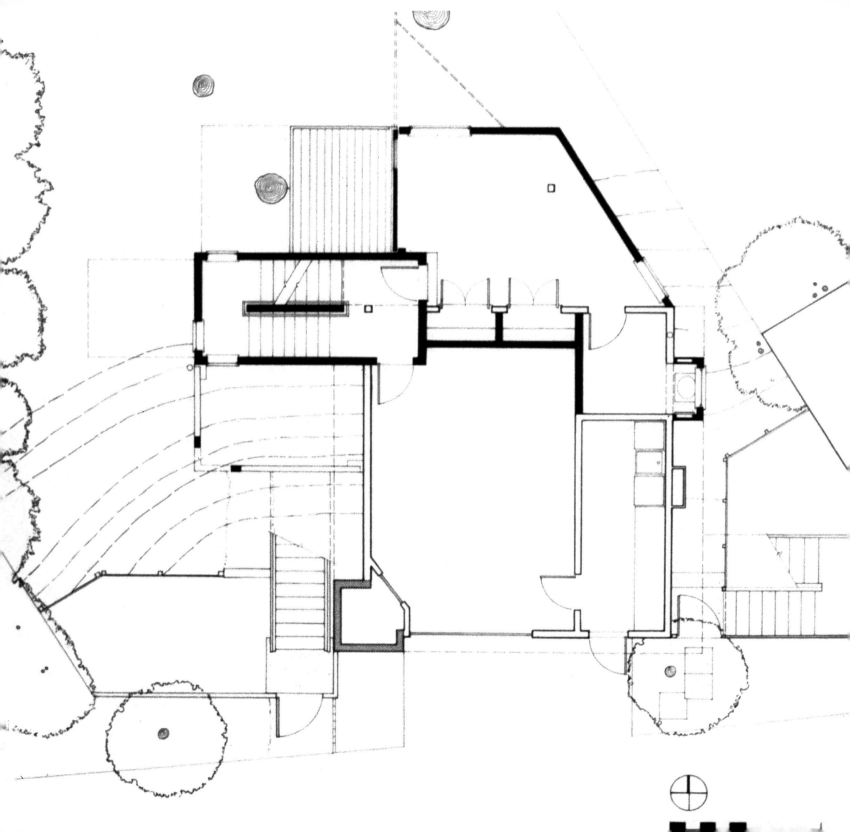

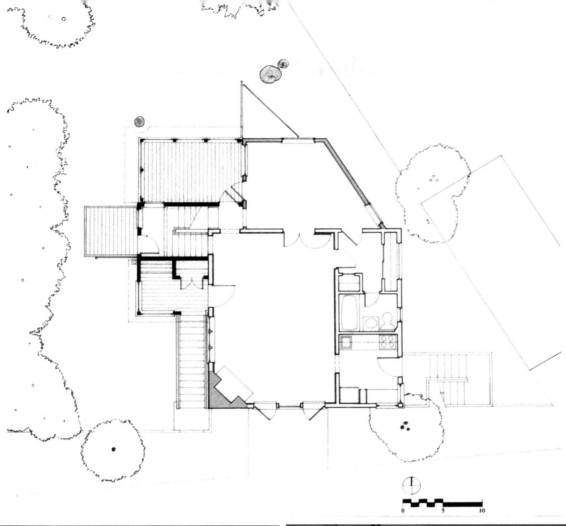

Located in an area known as "Camp del Robert" in the town of Meranges in the Catalan Pyrénees, this mountain hut was designed for a famliy of three that occasionally spends some periods in the Cerdanya during casual weekends, winters, and short periods of summer holidays. The site is found on the top of the village from where the house would be seen and where it would crown the village as seen from the distance.

The strict town policy for new buildings has been successfully applied as far as traditional materials are concerned. In order to satisfy the owners' desire for minimalism, the architect gathered the different day spaces in the single space under the roof with the longest dimension in the plan, creating a house where all of the living spaces remain integrated.

House in Les Meranges

Year: 1999 • Location: Camp del Robert, Les Meranges (village), Girona, Spain • Floor Area: 1,183.60 square feet •
Architects: Jorge Álvarez Alçón, Ernest Minguillón Moure/Álvarez-Minguillón Arquitectes • Photographer: Núria Fuentes

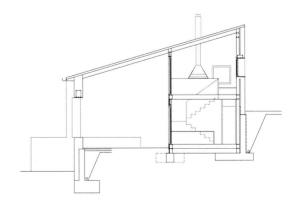

Can you describe briefly the design concept behind the project and the reason for its compactness?

In the beginning, we were interested in keeping the image of the building closed most of the time, so that it would crown the village with its small size. We tried to draw on farm buildings, built with stone walls and a south-facing wooden façade, that are used to store dried straw. On the other hand, we needed to increase the whole scale and make the house look bigger. To do this, the main façade had to have closed windows with wooden doors, which would create a hermetic, continuous plane that eliminated any reference to the building's use. We also used the porch as an integrated element, making a large space in the plan to make it appear bigger than it would have had we used a more domestic approach.

What is the most striking feature/element of this project that you believe makes it unique from other small-scale houses?

The most striking element of this building is the south façade—a unique wood plan that destroys the dimension and uses the building's references.

If you were to lay down Five Commandments for effective compact architectural design, what would these be? Relate also how each commandment is fulfilled in the project.

1) Have a close environment integration. In this project, the environment is integrated with the porch, which adds to the final volume of the building; also, the rhythm of the windows in the living room appears close to the landscape.

2) Abide by simplicity and geometric abstraction— the space arrangement is as simple as possible and the façades are turned into mere abstract planes.

3) Apply austerity in the dimensions, materials, and construction details—the project merely combined stonewall and wood.

4) Practice multi-use of spaces—the kitchen, dining room, living room, and stairs are combined under one roof, making the space big and unique.

5) Add several spaces in a bigger one—the vestibule consists of the stairs, playing room, laundry, storage, etc.

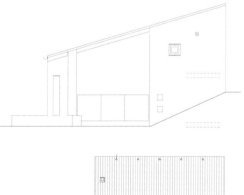

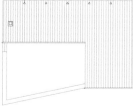

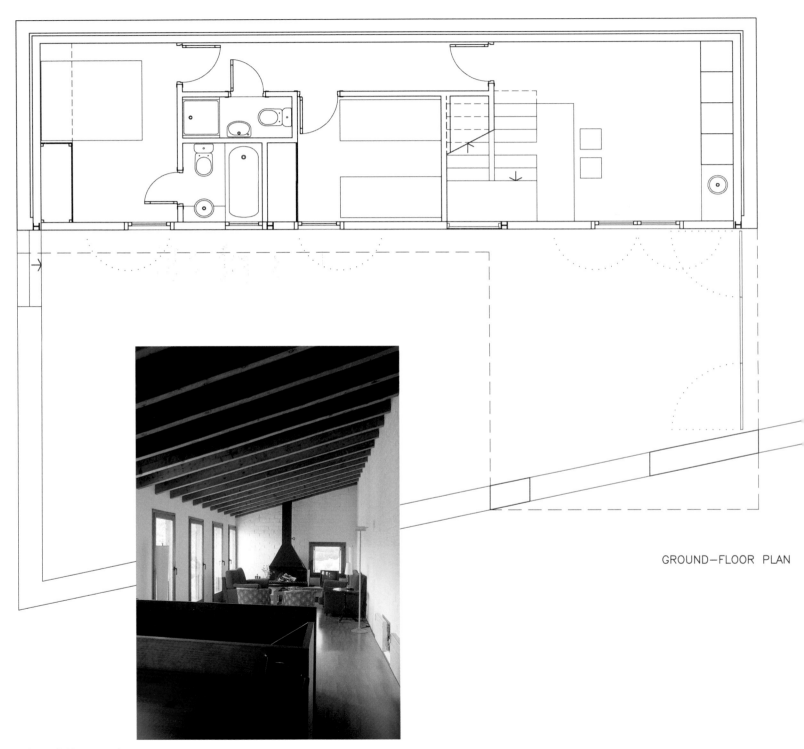

GROUND—FLOOR PLAN

The façades are turned into mere abstract planes.

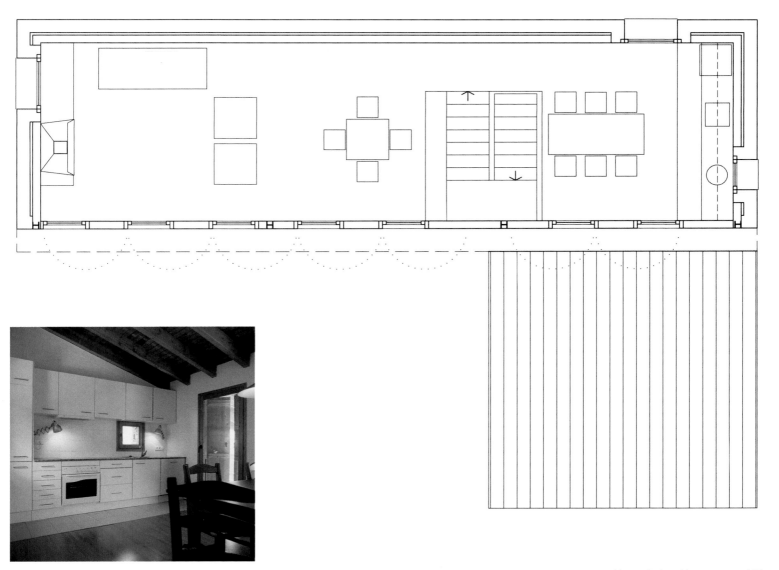

The site for this house is a narrow, linear garden behind an existing restaurant on Railway Street in Navan, Ireland. It was designed in response to the clients' particular requirements: they needed to be near to but separate from their work. They had been living over the restaurant and had used an existing courtyard—the hollowed-out shell of a disused workshop—as an outdoor room.

The house is organized around three courtyards, with external circulation between the living and sleeping zones. The living space and the bedroom tower are positioned on either side of the footprint of the former workshop. Story-height retaining walls hold back the higher-level neighbors' gardens on either side of the court; the living room roof is situated on the same level as the adjoining gardens. The cast-in-place cranked roof gives the living space a cavelike character. The cave, courtyard, and tower are the constituent elements of this concrete house, excavated from the existing conditions of the site.

Hudson House

Year: 1997 • Location: Railway Street, Navan, Ireland • Floor Area: 1,183.60 square feet •
Architects: Sheila O'Donnell, John Tuomey, Fiona McDonald/O'Donnell + Tuomey Architects • Photographer: John Searle

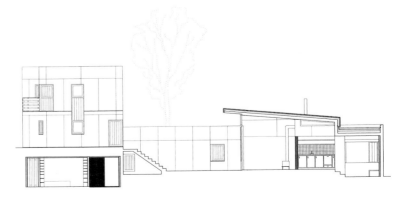

The roof gives the living space
a cave like character.

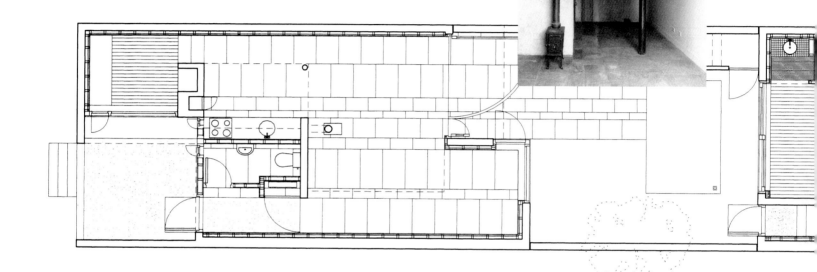

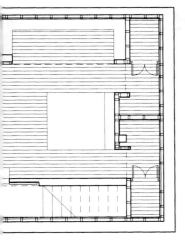

Can you describe briefly the design concept behind the project and the reason for its compactness?
The two-part house opens onto a sunken courtyard on a restricted site.

What is the most striking feature/element of this project that you believe makes it unique from other small-scale houses?
It is a combination of carved out space and cast-in-place construction.

If you were to lay down Five Commandments for effective compact architectural design, what would these be? Relate also how each commandment is fulfilled in the project.
1) Attain conceptual clarity.
2) Think of formal economy.
3) Have spatial flexibility.
4) Maintain internal/external interdependence.
5) Create complex simplicity.

The goal of this project was the creation of a painting studio at home for the painter Carol Moore, so that she could better balance the demands of her work and a growing young family. The home is on the ground floor portion of a large, stone-built Victorian villa set within mature gardens in Balloch, on the north side of the river Clyde from Glasgow. The task was to capture different views of the surrounding nature, which forms the inspiration for much of the artist's work.

Moore Clark Studio

Year: 1999 · Location: Balloch, Scotland, UK · Floor Area: 430.40 square feet · Architect: Christopher Platt/Studio KAP · Photographer: Keith Hunter

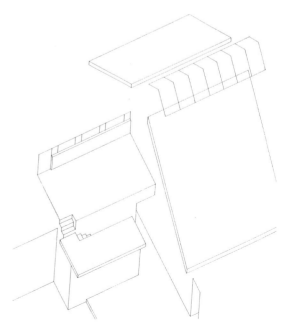

Can you describe briefly the design concept behind the project and the reason for its compactness?

The scheme consists of a series of three decks (one at ground level and two on the upper) on which activities take place. The highest deck is for painting and messy work, the middle one for cleaner, computer-based work, and the lowest is a social and family space arranged for dining and lounging. These are sheltered by a generous slated and boarded tent. The painting deck is positioned directly above the existing kitchen, and this establishes the basis for the scheme and the spatial compactness.

We are interested in the "song of a material."

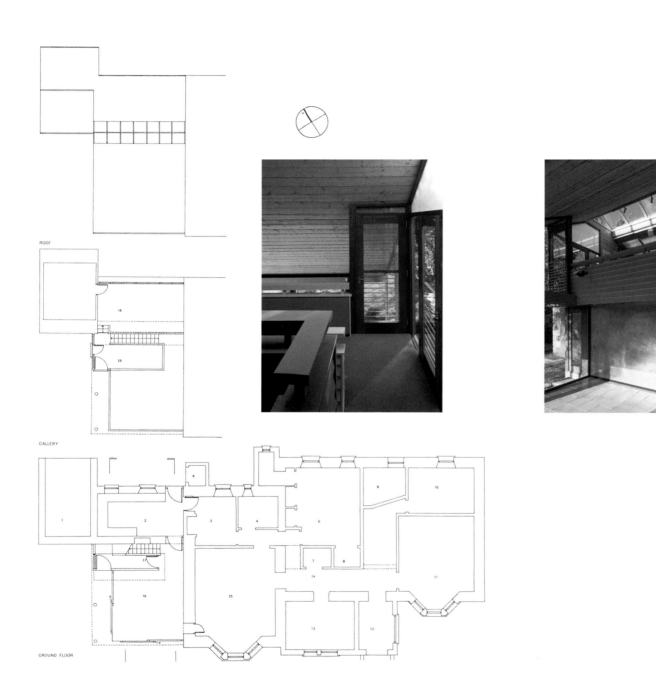

ROOF

GALLERY

GROUND FLOOR

What is the most striking feature/element of this project that you believe makes it unique from other small-scaled houses?

The most striking feature is the section and how it is exploited to create a number of different places within one space.

The existing stone structure was essential to creating as economic a structure as possible. We are also interested in the "song of a material" (the stone's intrinsic character) and its ability to contribute directly or indirectly to architectural character. Thus, a collection of steel channels and posts are built into and onto the existing thick, stone walls. Bright sunlight enters from the open slot at ridge level. Muted light, filtered through the surrounding mature trees, enters through the large glazed screens at the side and also through a narrow horizontal slit at the upper level, while a watery light, softened by the large lawn area found immediately outside, enters at low level through big, sliding glazed screens. These connect the lower space immediately with the garden.

If you were to lay down Five Commandments for effective compact architectural design, what would these be? Relate also how each commandment is fulfilled in the project.

1) Exploit the section to allow different types of daylight in and different types of views out—bright, soft, and dappled light enters the space from above, the side, and below either directly or as reflected in the grass and trees.
2) Create different places within one overall space to maximize different experiences of being there—the use of galleries at slightly different levels under the large, unifying roof, which overlooks the dining space below, allows different architectural events taking place at the same time.
3) Pay attention to detail, since in small spaces you are closer to details than in large spaces. Mostly exterior-quality materials used in their unfinished state creates the character. The particular design of the boarded galleries and their chunky handrail helps contain each gallery space, while allowing visual connections further afield.

4) Carefully consider what elements (furniture or storage) can be built-in and what can/should be freestanding—utilize throwaway space under the stairs or within thick, framed out walls for shelves.
5) Design elements or spaces that can solve more than one problem at once, in other words, "Kill as many birds with one stone as possible." The galleries are carefully dimensioned to be able to accommodate sleeping if their uses change over time. They are spaces grown-up children could use to study in.

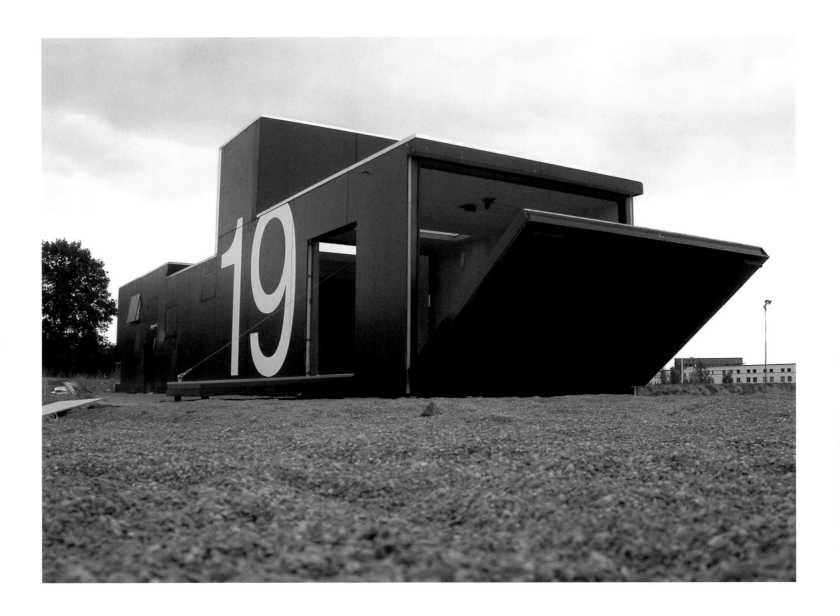

Various "Artists in Residence" were invited by the municipality of Utrecht to stay and work for a limited period of time in the newly built city extension of Leidsche Rijn. Their task was to observe and react to the growing and rapidly changing site from various perspectives. The accommodation itself, a mobile studio, is part of the municipal art program.

The house was commissioned with a tight, lump-sum budget; but rather than minimizing size and weight, as one would expect when designing a mobile home, the aim of the architects was to maximize its dimensions and functionality. Despite its mobility, it is big, robust, and durable. The object consists of one long space that can be subdivided into different interior and exterior spaces. It is a house that is to be used in many ways: as a hotel room, a studio, or a hospitable dwelling with a big table, good daylight, and as much privacy as one needs.

House No19

Year: 2003 • Location: Utrecht, the Netherlands • Floor Area: 774.72 square feet • Architects: Mechthild Stuhlmacher, Rien Korteknie/Korteknie Stuhlmacher Architecten, BikvanderPol (collaborators) •
Photographers: Mechthild Stuhlmacher, Rien Korteknie, Christian Kahl

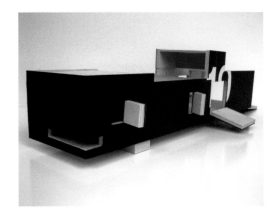

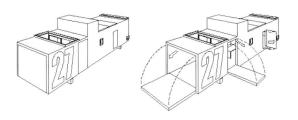

Can you describe briefly the design concept behind the project and the reason for its compactness?

The construction of the project is simple: the walls, floor, and roof have been made entirely of solid, laminated sheets of European softwood, stabilized by simple steel frames. The object is stable enough to be lifted and transported in one piece—sturdy, heavy, and environmentally sound. Its dimensions just allow for transportation on public roads. During transportation, the object is completely closed and is lit from above. If the large shutters are opened, the introvert house gets a completely different character. The shutters turn into terraces, ramps, and podia. The timber interior then becomes part of its surroundings and the artist presents himself and his work to the city.

What is the most striking feature/element of this project that you believe makes it unique from other small-scale houses?

Many small-scale houses are unique objects. The only way to be successful in this scale of work, or at least to build one distinct small house, is to attain personal commitment. The house is strikingly simple: the uncovered, rough structural material determines the quality of the space. The daylight inside is especially characteristic, beautiful, and lively. Due to the large shutters, the inside relates to the outside space in an exceptionally direct and powerful way.

If you were to lay down Five Commandments for effective compact architectural design, what would these be? Relate also how each commandment is fulfilled in the project.

1) Have a personal commitment between the client and the architect without counting the hours spent on the project.
2) Have a strong relationship among the construction method, the materials used, and the architectural idea.
3) Attain architectural discipline to limit the amount of formal and structural ideas.
4) Collaborate with craftsmen who enjoy the work.
5) Have a tight but reasonable budget.

The inside relates to the outside space in an exceptionally direct and powerful way.

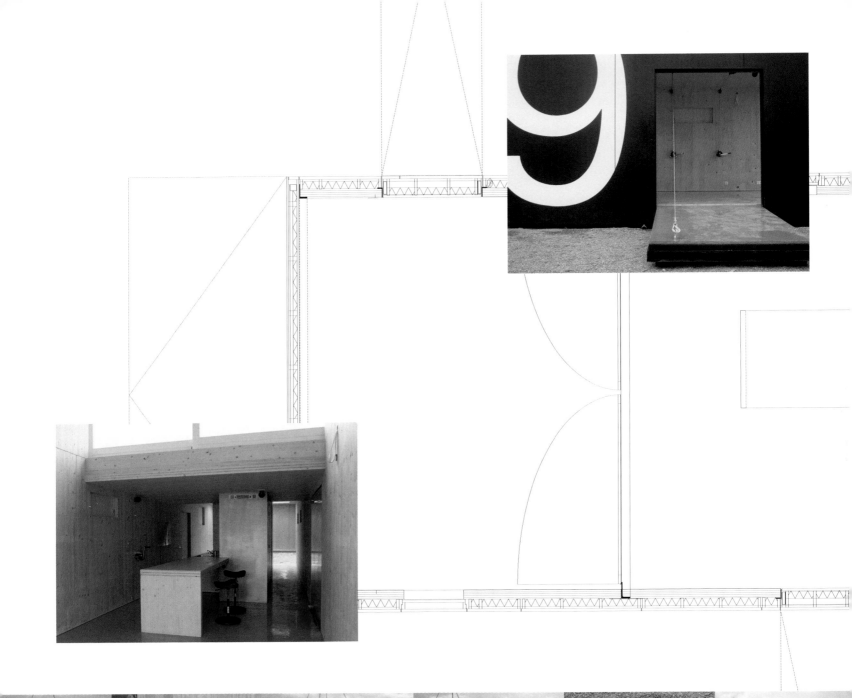

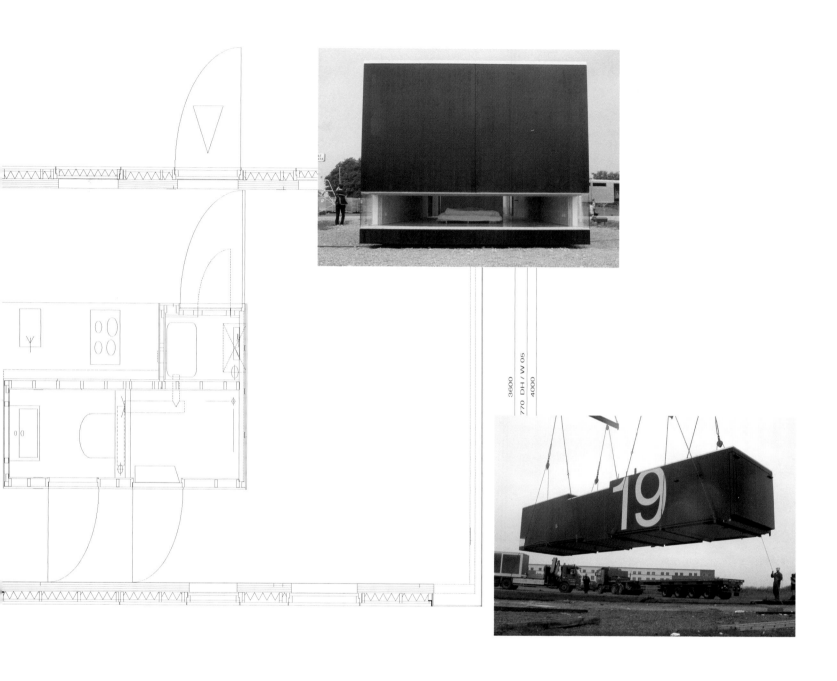

3600

770 DH / W 05

4000

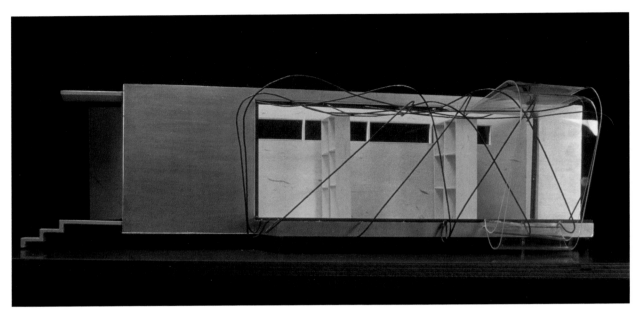

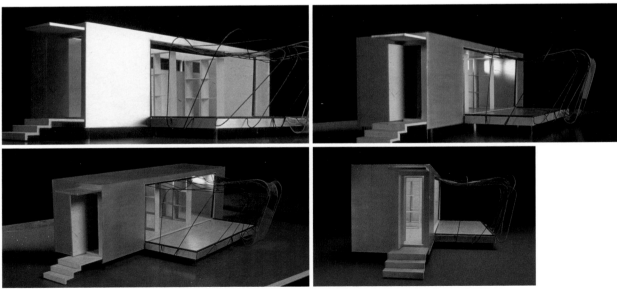

Snail is a prototype of a moveable small house that can be adapted to an urban environment. The project is based on an entry that received second prize in the Dreaming for the Future idea competition held at Helsinki, Finland, in 2001. The objective was to study the problems of an easily transported, low-cost small house suited to the urban environment.

Snail can be used as a permanent home or on a temporary basis, for example, during business trips or vacations. It is more than just a home: it is your office; it is a device you use for living; it is clothing you wear for protection. It is a capsule you take everywhere.

Snail

Year: 2004 • Location: Finland • Floor Area: 80.70–591.80 square feet • Architect: Markku Hedman/Architects M.H. Coop • Photographer: Markku Hedman

Can you describe briefly the design concept behind the project and the reason for its compactness?
The Snail consists of a shell, a skin, and an infill system. The supporting structures and measures of the shell are based on universally standardized container units that can be covered with steel, aluminium, copper, plastic, or wood. All elements can easily be changed, replaced, or repaired. During transportation, the shell is closed, and the skin and infill system are placed inside. When the Snail is used, a protecting hatch is opened, and a transparent, moldable, and inflatable three-layered skin is revealed, fitting the house into any kind of space.

The flexible infill system consists of furniture that slides along ceiling rails, toilet units, and varied technical installations, which can be rearranged in only a couple of minutes. It can also be connected to the existing infrastructures.

What is the most striking feature/element of this project that you believe makes it unique from other small-scale houses?
Snail is a new type of dwelling concept that is modular, moveable, and transformable. It is an urban chameleon with a moldable skin that can change its color and appearance and adjust its shape and size to blend into the environment.

The Snail is used to examine the use of information technology as well as the implementation of "open building" and "design for all" principles in housing design and construction. By individualizing space, the Snail challenges the prevailing typology of residential buildings and planned solutions, transforming itself to meet the actual and varying needs of a complex reality.

If you were to lay down Five Commandments for effective compact architectural design, what would these be? Relate also how each commandment is fulfilled in the project.
1) Challenge standard and universal design—emphasize the applicability and uniformity in the modernization of a residence.
2) Define dwellings by technical and economical interests and products standardized to the smallest detail by establishing the ways to arrange and measure furniture and fittings.
3) Use maximum manual skills, freedom, and independence for small-scale architecture.
4) Consider the client's wishes, the site's special qualities, and the unique opportunities of small houses.
5) Explore lighting, ventilation, temperature, safety and privacy controls, and spatial properties that change from a static to a self-organizing structure.

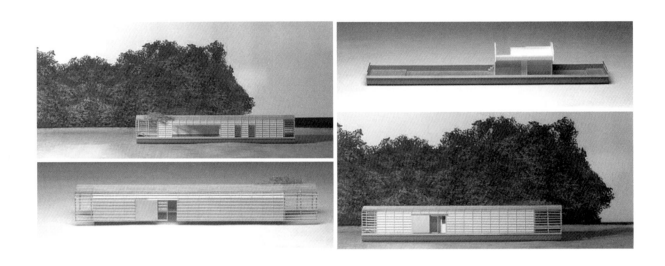

The boathouse, situated on a river near Paris, is a floating studio and lodge designed to house an artist in residence. The artist's life and work are organized by different spaces that are neither defined nor permanent, creating a multifunctional living space where one can both live and work.

Floating House

Year: 2003 • Location: Chatou, France • Floor Area: 1,000.68 square-foot house, 258.24 square-foot terrace • Designers: Ronan Bouroullec, Erwan Bouroullec/Ronan and Erwan Bouroullec • Architects: Jean-Marie Finot/Groupe Finot, Denis Daversin/Daversin Engineering • Photographer: Paul Tahon

Can you describe briefly the design concept behind the project and the reason for its compactness?
The house is composed of a barge and polyester strips (like the skin of a boat), which are assembled to build the roof and walls. Two glass façades face the terrace and the river. A wooden trellis covers and dresses up the overall assembly of the house. The interior is fully made of the same wood for the floor, ceiling, etc., except for the bathroom. The fixed skeleton of the structure is kept as open as possible by creating a central technical part that includes the kitchen and the bath. On both sides, there are two large rooms: one small that is intended for a bedroom, and the bigger one that is undefined.

What is the most striking feature/element of this project that you believe makes it unique from other small-scale houses?
The structure of the house shaped as a boat is its most unique feature. In this project, the size of the boat had to be dealt with, for it had to remain quite small due to transportation reasons. On the other hand, the river is infinite. The vegetation that should expand and develop around the building integrates it with the wooded landscape of the riverside and preserves the residents' intimacy at the same time.

If you were to lay down Five Commandments for effective compact architectural design, what would these be? Relate also how each commandment is fulfilled in the project.
1) Fit the house exactly into the desired area by using the small space more rationally in order to gain the maximum space possible.
2) Do not use too many walls, for the inside skeleton has to be reduced to its simplest form. Different kinds of functions can take place in the same room (dining, work, party, single life activities).
3) Do not use too many different visual materials for a small environment.
4) Have enough light and windows to escape a small space and to open the house to the outside.
5) Use strong finishes and materials to support different occupations in a small space.

The Villa Noailles is a cultural center in the south of France. The building in which the center is located was built by Robert Mallet-Stevensen. The curator of the villa commissioned four designers to make proposals for an artist's habitat, a space in which an artist could isolate himself to sleep, eat, and work. So far, the cabin exists only as a project concept. We present here two case studies for this project: the Artist's Cabin by Delo Lindo and Cabane Noailles 2002 by Radi Designers.

Artist's Cabin

Year: 2002 • Location: Hyères, Villa Noailles, France • Floor Area: 215.20 square feet • Architects: Fabien Cagani, Laurent Matras/Delo Lindo

Can you describe briefly the design concept behind the project and the reason for its compactness?
We were asked to create a small living space for artists, a place of retreat with basic interior functions (sleeping, relaxing, and eating). We soon came up with the idea of creating a cabinlike space. The special scale of the cabin is due to its functional requirements, as well as the size, powerful character, and proximity of Villa Noailles' impressive architecture, with which it contrasts.

What is the most striking feature/element of this project that you believe makes it unique from other small-scale houses?
The cabin's design was linked with the two following ideas: assembly in its most fundamental sense, by associating objects or materials in order to create a shelter; and at the same time, the choice of assembly should reflect the given environmental conditions, being either natural or artificial.

The cabin can be a graduation of possibilities, ranging from half-open to completely open. The cabin consists of a system that adopts traditional architectural elements, all of which are standard and mass-produced catalogue products—doors, windows, etc., are used in such a systematic and repetitive manner that they become the unique components of the architecture.

If you were to lay down Five Commandments for effective compact architectural design, what would these be? Relate also how each commandment is fulfilled in the project.
The artist's cabin for the Villa Noailles was a very specific project. It is the only "compact house" we have ever designed. To decline a list of rules from one single experience seems difficult. The "five rules" are dependent on the precise environment, and in our opinion cannot really be generalized.

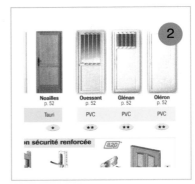

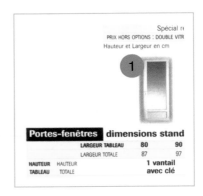

This modest wooden cabin is bordered by an intriguing terrace, which hints at the cabin's true nature: it can literally open into two parts. In this way, the user can be inside and outside at the same time.

The interior blends into the garden, and the space opens. The floor spreads out, and the chairs, table, and kitchen are exposed. The fireplace takes the center stage, as it becomes a barbeque in the center of the terrace. The bed borders the airy space, highlighting this spacious living structure where the borders of the home are pushed to the limit.

Cabane Noailles 2002

Year: 2002 • Location: Hyères, Villa Noailles, France • Floor Area: 215.20 square-foot house, 322.80 square-foot terrace •
Architects: Florence Doléac, Laurent Massaloux, Olivier Sidet, Robert Stadler/Radi Designers • Photographer: Robert Stadler

Can you describe briefly the design concept behind the project and the reason for its compactness?
We wanted to build a house in the densest manner possible, which could permit the users to extend their space of life, under the sun and with friends.

The cabin is split into two parts, and one half is hinged and mounted on wheels. The floor and terrace follow the path of the wheeled half. Differently colored zones demarcate the stops that it makes.

Facing the south, the cabin looks towards the sea, inspiring tranquility. When the door is unbolted, the occupant gives a strenuous push, opening up the hinged part of the house. Playing with the space, he can decide the degree of openness as he wishes, depending on the amount of light he needs. The wall acts like a screen, taking the cupboard and the fireplace.

What is the most striking feature/element of this project that you believe makes it unique from other small-scale houses?
The most striking element is most probably the hinge, which is the open element that unifies the concrete floor.

If you were to lay down Five Commandments for effective compact architectural design, what would these be? Relate also how each commandment is fulfilled in the project.
1) Attain flexibility.
2) Establish an opening to the outside.
3) The house should be "chipper."
4) The atmosphere should be comfortable.
5) All design elements should be fully integrated with each other.

"Living is nowadays less static and less continuous than in the past. A more nomadic lifestyle especially experienced by people living in urban zones and larger cities also influences the constitution of daily objects like furniture, technical installation and accessories. Most smaller objects are used more ambulant and consequently, larger objects like furniture need to be designed for flexible use. The future capacities of furniture will be linked to functional options like knock-down concepts, condensed volume-transportation, reconfiguration of elements, lightness, addition in steps. As younger urbanists change their homes quite often, furniture need to be modular systems."

— *Werner Aisslinger*,
Studio Aisslinger

Our daily lives are often dictated by the pieces of objects we sit on, write on, sleep on and store things into. Selecting the proper furniture and learning to actually like it almost becomes an art. In a mini house style, the choice of furnishings poses an even greater challenge. A tiny room of cluttered chairs, tables, beds and storage cabinets can transform into a modest and refined abode with just the right tinge of design creativity and technique. In this chapter, we present to you a wide showcase of our internationally selected furniture from the world's most prominent designers, created for comfort and stylish living in small spaces. These are grouped into four categories:
Stacking Makes Space
Variety Adds Versatility
Foldable Is Flexible
Modules Create Mobility

FURNITURE FOR COMPACT LIVING

Stacking makes space

The smartest solution to space limitation is vertical stacking. For storage and easy transport, lightness of material and portability enhance comfort living.

My 083
Michael Young/UK, Magis S.p.A.
low tables

Bar Sport Sgabello
Marco Ferreri/Italy, Magis S.p.A.
bar stools

Yuyu
Stefano Giovannoni/Italy
Magis S.p.A.
L42.5 x W44 x H50-60
air molded chairs

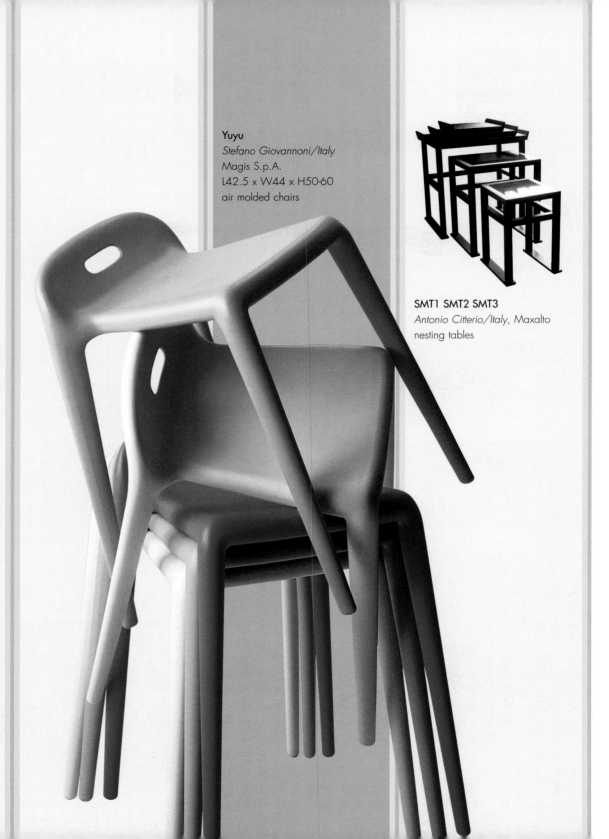

SMT1 SMT2 SMT3
Antonio Citterio/Italy, Maxalto
nesting tables

Air One/Air Two
Ross Lovegrove/UK, EDRA
light armchairs and stools

780/783
Gianfranco Frattini/Italy
Cassina/Photo: Aldo Ballo
beechwood tables

>>

Snoozy
Nick Crosbie/Paul Crofts/UK
Inflate Design Ltd.
foldable system bed

FPE 8009
Ron Arad/UK, Kartell
"fantastic plastic elastic" chairs

Stacking makes space — 177

Foldable
is
flexible

To use now or later, foldable and collapsible pieces answer the need for a temporary interior setting. For outdoor use, such function can be indispensable.

Aida Table
Richard Sapper/Germany, Magis S.p.A.
round folding tables

Clino Once Again
Mario Mazzer/Italy, Magis S.p.A.
retractable wall table

Fold Wrap Chair
Munenori Ueyama/Japan
Hula Hoop Design Factory
wrap-around chairs

Battista
Antonio Citterio/Italy, Oliver Löw/
Germany, Kartell
extendable trolleys

Coso
Enzo Berti/Italy
Magis S.p.A.
collapsible shelf unit

Tecnotable
Christophe Pillet/France, Magis S.p.A.
foldable-top table

Modules create mobility

"One plus one equals three," is a practical guide for designing modular pieces that can be combined, grouped and moved from one corner to the other. Vertical and horizontal space manipulation can be endless.

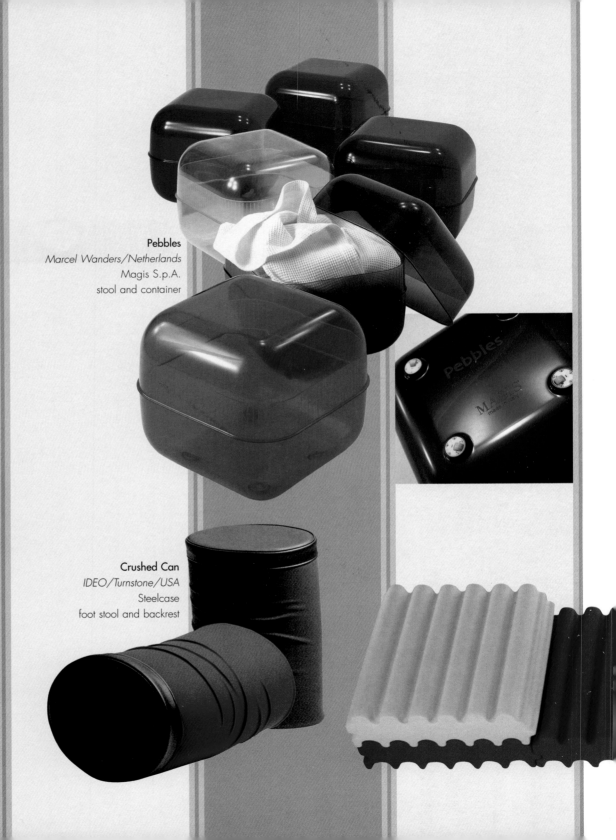

Pebbles
Marcel Wanders/Netherlands
Magis S.p.A.
stool and container

Kick
Toshiyuki Kita/Japan
Cassina/Photo: Aldo Ballo
pivoting low table

Crushed Can
IDEO/Turnstone/USA
Steelcase
foot stool and backrest

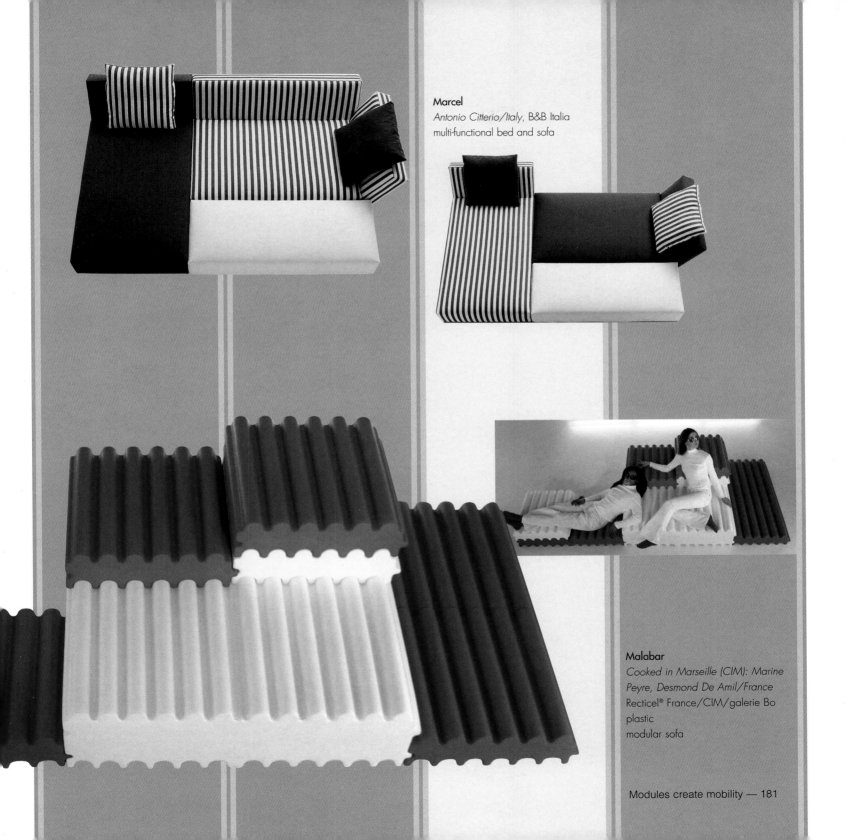

Marcel
Antonio Citterio/Italy, B&B Italia
multi-functional bed and sofa

Malabar
*Cooked in Marseille (CIM): Marine
Peyre, Desmond De Amil/France
Recticel® France/CIM/galerie Bo*
plastic
modular sofa

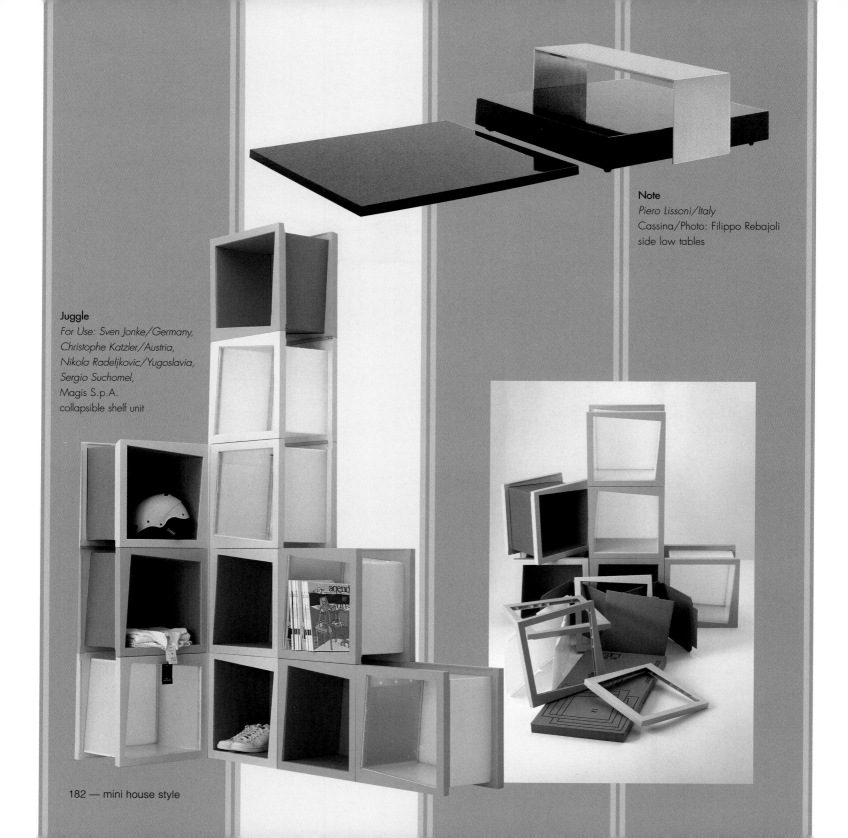

Note
Piero Lissoni/Italy
Cassina/Photo: Filippo Rebajoli
side low tables

Juggle
For Use: Sven Jonke/Germany,
Christophe Katzler/Austria,
Nikola Radeljkovic/Yugoslavia,
Sergio Suchomel,
Magis S.p.A.
collapsible shelf unit

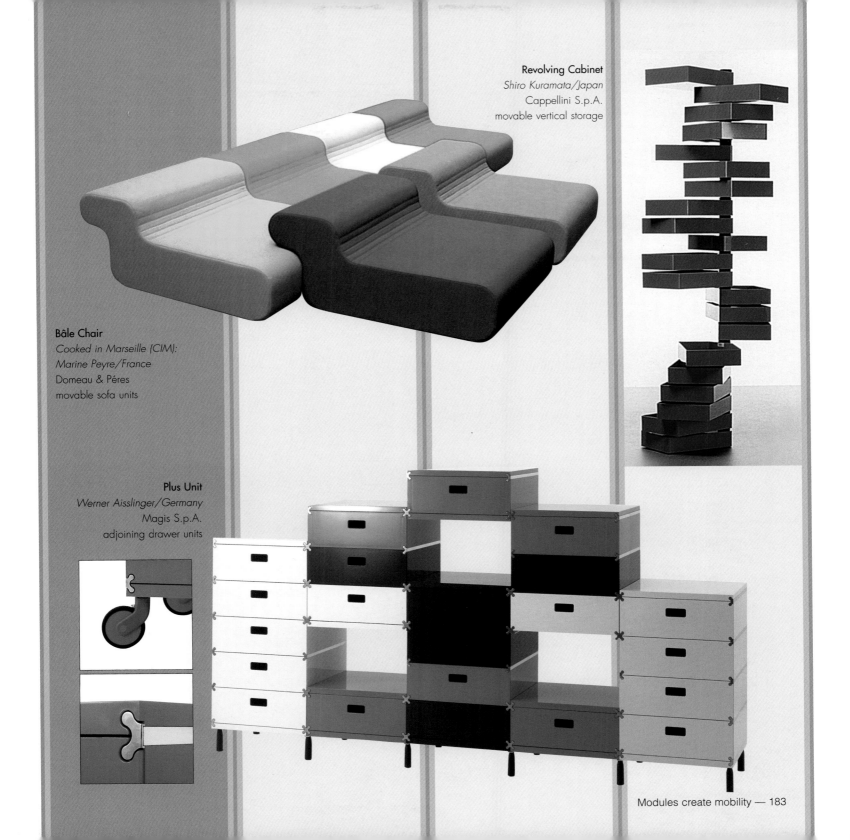

Revolving Cabinet
Shiro Kuramata/Japan
Cappellini S.p.A.
movable vertical storage

Bâle Chair
Cooked in Marseille (CIM):
Marine Peyre/France
Domeau & Péres
movable sofa units

Plus Unit
Werner Aisslinger/Germany
Magis S.p.A.
adjoining drawer units

Modules create mobility — 183

Variety
adds
versatility

What technology and creativity can produce together can be magical. Furniture pieces convert into multi-purpose functional creations that bring about the element of surprise.

2073 Box
Olaf von Bohr/Austria
Gedy S.p.A.
stool as chair and storage

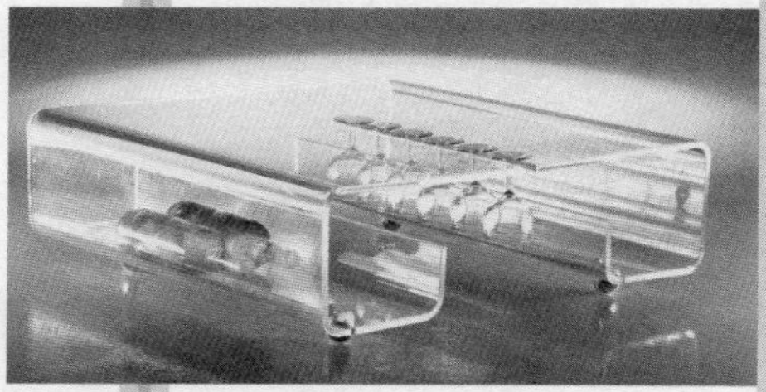

WINE TABLE
Cooked in Marseille (CIM):
Marine Peyre/France
CIM/Réaplastic® France
dual-purpose wine table

Sleep Sofa
Primitive+: Takeshi Hada, Shigeaki Watanabe, Masaya, Yokogawa/ Japan, Baden Baden
multi-purpose sofabed

Wink
Toshiyuki Kita/Japan
Cassina S.p.A./Photo: Andrea Zani
convertible lounge

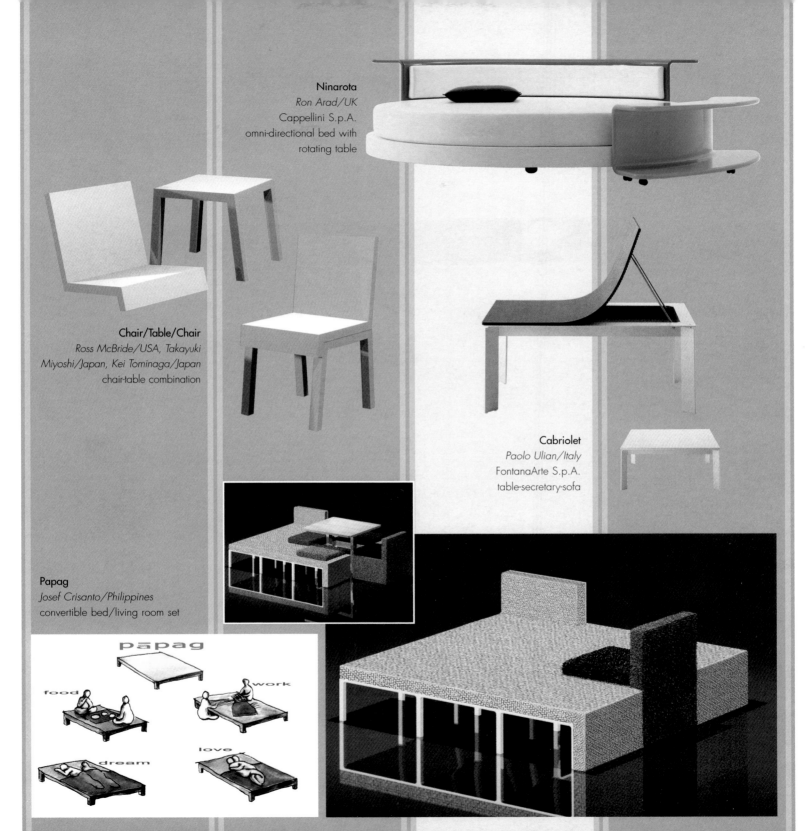

Ninarota
Ron Arad/UK
Cappellini S.p.A.
omni-directional bed with
rotating table

Chair/Table/Chair
*Ross McBride/USA, Takayuki
Miyoshi/Japan, Kei Tominaga/Japan*
chair-table combination

Cabriolet
Paolo Ulian/Italy
FontanaArte S.p.A.
table-secretary-sofa

Papag
Josef Crisanto/Philippines
convertible bed/living room set

pāpag

food

work

dream

love

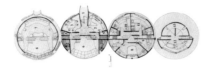
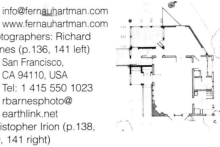

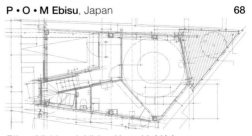

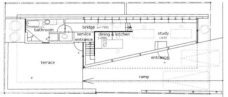
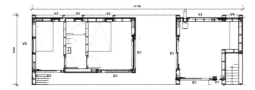
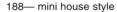
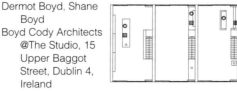

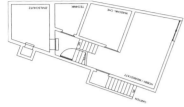

ACKNOWLEDGMENTS

Mini House Style in the Making

by Rico Komanoya

There are over a hundred thousand links in the internet in the search for "small house," "mini architecture," "compact living," "tiny residences," or other similar expressions pertaining to small-scale architecture, which proves that there is a wide, global dissatisfaction in today's living conditions. Although the concept of smallness and narrowness depends variably per environment and country, there is a common need to improve one's lifestyle and daily environment by using limited space effectively.

The **Mini House Style** project stemmed from the search of small-scale residences with absolutely less than eight hundred sixty square feet of floor space. Our original approach was to categorize each project into color, height, material, and structure, which play key criteria in making small and limited spaces look wider and more comfortable. However, we realized that we had omitted prospective projects from Europe, USA and Asia that did not meet our size preference even if they were highly impressive and overwhelming in terms of design. Perhaps, we had strictly confined our criteria to the target floor area without giving more importance to the spirit of "living small." The preliminary number of selected projects was apparently, not sufficient to complete a 192-page book project, while our deadline was fast approaching.

After requesting for a deadline extension, reviewing the existing projects, and discussing what factors should be added to offer an innovatively new look to the book, we decided to include prototype projects (**Snail, Floating House, Artist's Cabin, and Cabane Noailles 2002**) that presented new and unique concepts of thinking and living in mini spaces. As of this date, there have been no existing titles in the market that highlight this subject,which therefore, gave higher value to this book.

We also wanted to provide a "fun," creative, and artistic layout by overlapping interior shots on the actual floor plans. Although this bold design approach is often used for the client's better visual understanding of the layout, some readers may find it difficult to interpret the floor plans. Hence, they were inserted in the Index and Credits section for the architects' and designers' detailed reference.

In thanking all those who have made the production of this book possible, I would like to mention primarily Paco Asensio of LOFT International, who commissioned me to write and edit this book with almost no conditions. I had no word of gratitude for him when he first told me about this project in the London Book Fair in 2003, "Listen, Rico, I have this book idea and I want you to wrap it up for me." At that time, I also had a similar book idea in my mind and I revealed it to him saying, "Paco, I have one book project which I may be able to package myself for Loft International." I will never forget his smile when we both realized that we spoke of the same idea during the same moment. He had placed his tremendous trust on me to complete the project despite his nervousness toward the progress of the production that took longer than expected. I respect him greatly not only as a good and long-time friend in the publishing industry, but also as a professional who possesses valuable and innovative ideas.

Aurora Cuito, the talented editorial coordinator at Loft International, had been incredibly patient, and never displayed upset toward any kind of unforeseen "accident." She had always handled the communication and actual production professionally. For all that she had done for this book, I am grateful to her eternally.

We requested Rikuo Nishimori, head of NAA (Nishimori Architects and Associates), author of several architectural design titles, and one of the highly representative Japanese architects of his generation, to supervise the selection of our materials. The staff of NAA made tremendous efforts to re-select the projects during midway of the production. Without their help and professional advices, the completion of this book project would not be achieved. I would like to thank them from the bottom of my heart.

A special appreciation must be given to all the contributors of both mini houses and furniture, who took the concept of "smallness" actively and positively, and shared their excellent projects, time and effort, despite their extremely busy schedules. They taught us that small spaces do not offer any disadvantage to an architectural project, but rather represent the best condition for fulfilling a design spirit founded on unique ideas, creative talent, and motivation. Thank you all for giving us inspiration.

We wish to thank also the following people who provided us generous assistance in collaborating with the architects, designers and photographers, and procuring materials for the book: Annabel Gaitskell, Aurélie Geslin, Banu Ataman, Barbara Artico, Beba Michard, Burkhard Schelischansky, Carey Clouse, Chizko Mori, Christine Lensch, Claudia Cappelleti, Constance Guisset, Corrie Zeeuw, M.D. van Arum-Van Eeuwijk/Delft University of Technology, Cristiana Bernardini, Cristina Sacilotto, Dublin Institute of Technology, Elena Foggini, Federica Fratoni, Fiona Mackenzie-Jenkin, Fiorella Villa, Francesca Simen, Fujiko Suda, Gabriella De Biase, Gareth Morris, Gunilla Antas/Department of Architecture, Helsinki University of Technology, Ilaria Biancalani, Isabella Colombo, Jefferey Schneider, Kathryn Meghen/Royal Institute of Architects of Ireland, Kazuhiro Takeuchi, Laura Confalonieri, Lise Steiness/Royal Academy of Fine Arts School of Architecture, Copenhagen, Louise Barber, Manabu Aritsuka, Marc Duflot, Marcelle Labbé/Intramuros SA, Maristella Bonalumi, Mari Mizuno, Masumi Enomoto, Monica Mazzei, Pascale Gibon, Perrine Vigneron, Ryan Kennihan, Susanne Ott, Susie Carson, Tiziana Croce, University of Strathclyde/ Department of Architecture, and Yasuyuki Okazaki.

My gratitude also goes to Keiko Kitamura for her generous English translation of the Japanese material.

Lastly, I would like to give special credit to the members of ricorico who gave everything they could to the production of this book: Alma Reyes-Umemoto and Eiko Nishida. Alma made an enormous contribution by corresponding with more than sixty contributing architectural and design offices worldwide, obtaining the necessary permissions, and copy-editing interview texts and other sections of this book. She conducted the research for the furniture contributions in the second chapter almost entirely by herself, and proved her skills as a material researcher that she could trace an e-mail correspondence dated 157 days ago without trouble or time effort.

As both art director and editorial designer, Eiko offered witty and innovative ideas throughout the pages of the book, and never compromised design to maintain the beauty of a standard page layout. She also created the playful icon drawings on the title page and the last page of the book. I thank you both for giving birth to ricorico's first impressive "baby" product.

September 2004

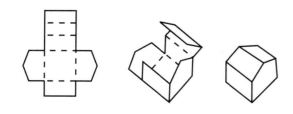